Sweet OLD-FASHIONED FAVOURITES

contents

Of all the tastes I remember with the most intense pleasure and nostalgia, those sweet old-fashioned favourites of childhood usually head the list. Here we have gathered together our most well known and best loved pastries, cakes, puddings, biscuits and other sweet treats. Many have a long history going back hundreds of years, while others are comparative youngsters, created by cakes shops in the last 30 or 40 years.

Pamela Clark

Food Director

cakes

Lemony cheesecakes, light and fluffy sponges, rich fruit and chocolate mixes, fairy cakes and teacakes – these are just some of the treats on the following pages. They're all guaranteed to reawaken the pleasure of baking, not to mention the delight of eating cake.

lemon cheesecake

Cheesecake was very popular in ancient Greece and it was probably the Romans, after their conquest of Greece, who introduced this delight to Western Europe. The lemon cheesecake variation appeared in English cookbooks as early as 1747.

250g packet plain sweet biscuits
125g butter, melted

FILLING
250g packet cream cheese, softened
400g can sweetened condensed milk
2 teaspoons grated lemon rind
1/3 cup lemon juice
1 teaspoon gelatine
1 tablespoon water

1 Lightly grease 20cm springform tin. Blend, process or crush biscuits finely; stir in butter. Using a flat-bottomed glass, press mixture evenly over base and side of prepared tin. Refrigerate crumb crust 30 minutes or until firm.

2 Pour filling into crumb crust; refrigerate several hours or until set. Serve with whipped cream, if desired.

filling Beat cream cheese in small bowl with electric mixer until smooth, beat in condensed milk, rind and juice; beat until smooth. Soften gelatine in water in cup, stir over hot water until dissolved. Stir gelatine mixture into lemon mixture.

SERVES 6 TO 8

recipe best made a day before serving
store covered, in refrigerator
freeze not suitable
microwave gelatine suitable

black forest cheesecake

The traditional Black Forest cake combination of cherries and rich chocolate came from Swabia in the Black Forest region of Germany. We have adapted the recipe to make this very popular cheesecake.

250g plain uniced chocolate biscuits, finely crushed
125g butter, melted
3 teaspoons gelatine
1/2 cup water
250g packet cream cheese, softened
3/4 cup caster sugar
1 tablespoon lemon juice
300ml carton thickened cream
425g can pitted black cherries

TOPPING

1 tablespoon cornflour
1 tablespoon caster sugar
1 tablespoon dark rum

1 Combine crumbs and butter in bowl, mix well; press over base and side of 20cm springform tin, refrigerate 30 minutes.

2 Sprinkle gelatine over water in cup, stand in small pan of simmering water, stir until dissolved; cool.

3 Beat cream cheese, sugar and juice in small bowl with electric mixer until smooth and creamy; transfer to large bowl.

4 Whip cream until soft peaks form, fold into cheese mixture; fold in gelatine mixture. Drain cherries, reserve 3/4 cup syrup for topping.

5 Spoon 1/3 of cheese mixture into crumb crust, top with 1/2 the cherries, then continue layering, ending with cheese mixture. Refrigerate several hours or until firm.

6 Spread topping over cheesecake, swirl gently into cheese mixture. Refrigerate until set.

topping Blend cornflour and sugar with reserved syrup in pan. Stir over heat until mixture boils and thickens, stir in rum; cool 10 minutes before using.

SERVES 6 TO 8

recipe can be made 2 days ahead
store covered, in refrigerator
freeze not suitable
microwave not suitable

baked cheesecake

Another variation on the ever-popular cheesecake, this has a lingering, light lemon taste and velvety texture. It's just one of the amazing variety of ways to make this favourite treat.

250g plain sweet biscuits
125g butter, melted

FILLING

3 x 250g packets cream
cheese, softened
1/2 cup caster sugar
3 eggs
3 teaspoons grated lemon
rind
1/4 cup lemon juice

1 Grease 20cm springform tin. Blend, process or crush biscuits finely; stir in butter. Using a flat-bottomed glass, press crumb mixture evenly over base and side of prepared tin; refrigerate 30 minutes or until firm.

2 Place springform tin on oven tray, pour filling into tin. Bake in moderately slow oven about 50 minutes, or until firm. Cool in oven with door ajar.

3 Cover cheesecake; refrigerate several hours or overnight before serving. Serve with fresh fruit, if desired.

filling Beat cheese and sugar in medium bowl with electric mixer until smooth. Add eggs 1 at a time, beating well after additions. Add rind and juice, beat until mixture is creamy.

recipe can be made 3 days ahead
store covered, in refrigerator
freeze suitable
microwave not suitable

cinnamon teacake

To make a light and fluffy teacake, it is important to cream the butter, essence, sugar and egg thoroughly until the mixture is as light and white as possible. Teacakes are best eaten warm from the oven.

60g butter
1 teaspoon vanilla essence
$2/3$ cup caster sugar
1 egg
1 cup self-raising flour
$1/3$ cup milk
10g butter, melted, extra
1 teaspoon ground cinnamon
1 tablespoon caster
**   sugar, extra**

1 Grease deep 20cm round cake pan, line base with paper; grease paper.

2 Beat butter, essence, sugar and egg in small bowl with electric mixer until light and fluffy.

3 Stir in sifted flour and milk, stir gently until smooth.

4 Spread mixture into prepared pan. Bake in moderate oven about 30 minutes. Turn onto wire rack, brush with extra butter, and sprinkle with combined cinnamon and extra sugar while hot. Serve warm with butter.

recipe best made on day of serving
store in airtight container
freeze suitable
microwave not suitable

date and walnut rolls

Only ever half fill the nut roll tins with mixture. Be careful of hot steam when turning out the cooked rolls.

1 cup (180g) chopped dates
60g butter
1 cup brown sugar, firmly packed
1 cup water
1/2 teaspoon bicarbonate of soda
1 egg, lightly beaten
1/2 cup chopped walnuts
2 cups self-raising flour

1 Grease two 8cm x 17cm nut roll tins.

2 Combine dates, butter, sugar and water in pan; stir over heat, without boiling, until sugar is dissolved. Bring to boil, remove from heat; cool.

3 Stir soda, egg, nuts and sifted flour into date mixture.

4 Spoon mixture evenly into prepared tins, replace lids. Bake, standing upright, in moderate oven about 40 minutes. Stand rolls 10 minutes before removing lids and turning onto wire rack to cool. Serve sliced with butter.

recipe can be made 2 days ahead
store in airtight container
freeze suitable
microwave not suitable

cherry cake

The subtle richness of almonds is brilliant with nice-to-bite cherry chunks.

180g butter, softened

1 teaspoon almond essence

3/4 cup caster sugar

3 eggs

2 cups self-raising flour

2 tablespoons packaged ground almonds

1/3 cup milk

1/2 cup sour cream

1 cup (210g) red glacé cherries, quartered

1 Grease deep 20cm round cake pan, line base with paper; grease paper.

2 Beat butter, essence and sugar in small bowl with electric mixer until light and fluffy; add eggs 1 at a time, beating well after additions.

3 Stir in sifted flour and almonds in 2 batches with milk and sour cream; stir in cherries.

4 Spread mixture into prepared pan; bake in moderate oven about 1¹/4 hours. Stand cake 3 minutes before turning onto wire rack to cool. Sprinkle with sifted icing sugar, if desired.

recipe can be made a day ahead

store in airtight container

freeze suitable

microwave not suitable

hummingbird cake

*A delectable American favourite, this moist cake is probably named after
the brilliant tiny American hummingbirds, whose staple diet is nectar.
Keep cake in the refrigerator if weather is wet or humid.*

1¹/₂ cups plain flour

1 cup caster sugar

¹/₂ teaspoon ground cinnamon

¹/₂ teaspoon bicarbonate of soda

3 eggs, lightly beaten

³/₄ cup oil

³/₄ cup chopped pecans or walnuts

2 cups mashed overripe bananas

¹/₂ cup undrained crushed
   pineapple in heavy syrup

CREAM CHEESE FROSTING

60g packaged cream
   cheese, softened

30g butter

1 teaspoon vanilla essence

1¹/₂ cups icing sugar

1 Lightly grease 23cm square slab pan, line base with paper; grease paper.

2 Sift flour, sugar, cinnamon and soda into large bowl. Stir in eggs, oil,
   nuts, banana and pineapple; stir until just combined.

3 Pour mixture into prepared pan; bake in moderate oven about 1 hour.
   Stand cake 10 minutes before turning onto wire rack to cool. Spread cold
   cake with cream cheese frosting.

cream cheese frosting Beat cream cheese, butter and essence in small
bowl with electric mixer until light and fluffy; gradually beat in sifted
icing sugar.

recipe can be made 3 days ahead

store in airtight container

freeze suitable

microwave not suitable

victoria sandwich

Among the many memorials to Queen Victoria are several culinary creations. The Victoria sandwich is undoubtedly the best known.

250g butter
1 teaspoon vanilla essence
1 cup caster sugar
4 eggs
2 cups self-raising flour
2 tablespoons jam
icing sugar

1 Grease 2 deep 20cm round cake pans, cover bases with paper; grease paper.

2 Beat butter, essence and sugar in small bowl with electric mixer until mixture is light and fluffy. Add eggs 1 at a time, beating well after additions.

3 Transfer mixture to large bowl, stir in sifted flour in 2 batches.

4 Spread mixture evenly in prepared pans; bake in moderate oven about 25 minutes. Turn cakes onto wire rack to cool. Join cakes with jam; dust cake with a little sifted icing sugar.

recipe best made on day of serving

freeze suitable
microwave not suitable

butter cake savvy

The eggs should be at room temperature and the butter softened but not melted. Always add any flavourings and essences in with the butter for maximum flavour. Stir flour and any liquid into the mixture in 2 batches to facilitate mixing; beat in eggs, 1 at a time, after breaking separately first in a saucer to make sure they're fresh.

marble cake

We've chosen the traditional children's party favourite combination of pink, white and chocolate, but there are many other equally attractive possibilities. Vary the colours and essence to suit yourself.

180g butter

1 teaspoon vanilla essence

3/4 cup caster sugar

2 eggs

1 1/2 cups self-raising flour

1/2 cup milk

pink food colouring

2 tablespoons cocoa

1 tablespoon milk, extra

ICING

90g butter

1 cup icing sugar

1 1/2 tablespoons milk

pink food colouring

1 Lightly grease 20cm ring cake pan, cover base with paper; grease paper.

2 Beat butter, essence and caster sugar in small bowl with electric mixer until mixture is light and fluffy. Add eggs 1 at a time, beating well after additions.

3 Transfer mixture to large bowl; fold in sifted flour and milk in 2 batches. Divide mixture evenly between 3 bowls.

4 Tint mixture pink in 1 bowl; mix well. Stir sifted cocoa and extra milk into second bowl; mix well. Drop spoonfuls of each of the 3 mixtures into prepared pan. Run a knife through cake mixture for a marbled effect.

5 Bake in moderate oven about 40 minutes. Stand cake 5 minutes before turning onto wire rack to cool.

6 Drop alternate spoonfuls of pink and white icing on top of cold cake. Using a spatula, swirl icing to give marbled effect.

icing Beat butter in small bowl with electric mixer until as white as possible; beat in sifted icing sugar and milk in 2 batches. Divide mixture between 2 bowls; use colouring to tint mixture pink in 1 bowl.

cake can be made a day ahead

store in airtight container

freeze suitable

microwave not suitable

devil's food cake

180g butter

1³/4 cups caster sugar

3 eggs

1¹/2 cups self-raising flour

¹/2 cup plain flour

¹/2 teaspoon bicarbonate of soda

²/3 cup cocoa

3 teaspoons dry instant coffee

¹/2 teaspoon red food colouring

¹/2 cup water

¹/2 cup milk

RICH CHOCOLATE FROSTING

60g dark chocolate

60g unsalted butter

1 Grease 2 deep 20cm round cake pans, line bases with paper; grease paper.

2 Beat butter and sugar in small bowl with electric mixer until light and fluffy; add eggs 1 at a time, beating well after additions.

3 Transfer mixture to large bowl, fold in sifted flours, soda and cocoa with combined coffee, colouring, water and milk, in 2 batches.

4 Pour mixture into prepared pans; bake in moderate oven about 45 minutes. Turn cakes onto wire rack to cool. Join cold cakes with whipped or mock cream, top with rich chocolate frosting.

rich chocolate frosting Combine chocolate and butter in heatproof bowl over pan of simmering water, stir until smooth. Remove from heat. Cool at room temperature until spreadable, stir occasionally while cooling.

uniced cake can be made 2 days ahead

store in airtight container

freeze uniced cake suitable

microwave icing suitable

dundee cake

180g butter, softened

3/4 cup caster sugar

5 eggs, lightly beaten

1½ cups plain flour

½ cup self-raising flour

½ teaspoon mixed spice

⅓ cup milk

1¼ cups (250g) raisins, chopped

1½ cups (250g) currants

1¼ cups (250g) sultanas

2 tablespoons mixed peel

⅓ cup glacé cherries, chopped

2 tablespoons blanched almonds

red glacé cherries, extra

blanched almonds, extra

1 tablespoon brandy

1 Line deep 20cm round cake pan with 3 layers of baking paper, bringing paper 5cm above edge of pan.

2 Beat butter, sugar, eggs, sifted dry ingredients and milk in large bowl with electric mixer on medium speed about 3 minutes or until mixture changes colour slightly. Stir in fruit and nuts, mix well.

3 Spread mixture into prepared pan, decorate top with extra cherries and nuts. Bake in slow oven about 3 hours. Brush hot cake with brandy; cover with foil, cool in pan.

recipe can be made a week ahead

store in airtight container

freeze suitable

microwave not suitable

gingerbread

Ginger, which is native to Asia, was first used in Western Europe more than 2000 years ago. Gingerbread is thought to be one of the world's earliest sweet cakes.

1 cup golden syrup

1 cup water

2/3 cup brown sugar, firmly packed

250g butter

3¹/₂ cups plain flour

1 teaspoon bicarbonate of soda

2 tablespoons ground ginger

1 teaspoon ground nutmeg

1 teaspoon ground cinnamon

LEMON ICING

60g butter, softened

2 teaspoons grated lemon rind

2 tablespoons lemon juice

2 cups icing sugar

1 Grease 23cm square slab pan, line base with paper; grease paper.

2 Combine golden syrup, water, sugar and butter in large pan, stir over heat until butter is melted, bring to boil; remove from heat. Cool to room temperature.

3 Stir sifted dry ingredients into butter mixture in 2 batches, beat gently until smooth.

4 Pour mixture into prepared pan; bake in moderately slow oven about 1¹/₄ hours. Stand cake 5 minutes before turning onto wire rack to cool. Spread cold cake with lemon icing.

lemon icing Beat butter and rind in small bowl with wooden spoon, gradually beat in juice and sifted icing sugar.

recipe can be made a week ahead

store in airtight container

freeze suitable

microwave not suitable

sultana cake

3 cups (500g) sultanas
250g butter
³/₄ cup caster sugar
5 eggs
2¹/₂ cups plain flour
¹/₄ cup self-raising flour
¹/₄ cup brandy

1 Grease deep 23cm round cake pan, line base with paper; grease paper.

2 Place sultanas in bowl, add enough hot water to cover; cover bowl, stand 2 hours.

3 Drain sultanas, spread sultanas on tray covered with absorbent paper or tea-towel; cover, stand overnight.

4 Have butter at room temperature. Beat butter and sugar in small bowl with electric mixer until light and fluffy; beat in eggs 1 at a time, beat until combined.

5 Transfer mixture to large bowl, stir in sifted flours, sultanas and brandy in 2 batches.

6 Spread mixture into prepared pan; bake in moderately slow oven about 1³/4 hours. Cover cake, cool in pan.
cake can be made a week ahead
store in airtight container
freeze suitable
microwave not suitable

fairy cakes

To make butterfly cakes, a variation of fairy cakes, cut the circle of cut-out cake in half, replace on the cream like wings. Decorate with silver cachous.

1¹/₂ cups self-raising flour
²/₃ cup caster sugar
125g butter, softened
3 eggs
¹/₄ cup milk
1 teaspoon vanilla essence
¹/₂ cup jam or lemon butter, approximately
300ml carton thickened cream

1 Line two 12-hole deep patty pans with paper cases.

2 Sift dry ingredients into small bowl of electric mixer, add butter, eggs, milk and essence. Beat on medium speed about 3 minutes or until mixture is smooth and slightly lighter in colour.

3 Drop 1¹/₂ tablespoons of mixture into prepared paper cases. Bake in moderate oven about 20 minutes or until lightly browned; cool in pans.

4 Using a fine-pointed knife, cut circles from tops of cakes about 1cm from edge and 1.5cm down into patty cakes.

5 Place about ¹/₂ teaspoon of jam or lemon butter into cavities of cakes, top with whipped cream. Place tops in position. Dust with sifted icing sugar.

MAKES 24

recipe can be prepared a day ahead
store keep unfilled cakes in airtight container; keep filled cakes, covered, in refrigerator
freeze unfilled cakes suitable
microwave not suitable

boiled fruit cake

Boiled fruit cake is quicker and less expensive to make than the traditional baked fruit cake. The boiled fruit mixture is best left to cool slowly overnight.

$2^2/_3$ **cups (500g) mixed dried fruit, chopped**
$1/_2$ cup water
1 cup brown sugar, firmly packed
125g butter
1 teaspoon mixed spice
$1/_2$ teaspoon bicarbonate of soda
$1/_2$ cup sweet sherry
1 egg, lightly beaten
1 cup plain flour
1 cup self-raising flour
blanched almonds
2 tablespoons sweet sherry, extra

1 Combine fruit, water, sugar, butter, spice and soda in large pan; stir over heat, without boiling, until sugar is dissolved and butter melted. Bring to boil; cover, simmer 5 minutes. Remove from heat, stir in sherry; cover, cool.

2 Grease deep 20cm round cake pan; line base and side with 2 thicknesses of paper, bringing paper 5cm above edge of pan.

3 Stir egg and sifted flours into fruit mixture.

4 Spread mixture into prepared pan, decorate top with almonds. Bake in moderately slow oven about 2 hours. Brush top of hot cake with extra sherry. Cover cake with foil, cool in pan.

recipe can be made 2 weeks ahead

store in airtight container

freeze suitable

microwave boiled fruit mixture suitable

ginger sponge

5 eggs, separated
³/₄ cup caster sugar
1 tablespoon golden syrup
¹/₃ cup self-raising flour
¹/₃ cup cornflour
3 teaspoons ground ginger
1 teaspoon ground cinnamon
2 teaspoons cocoa
³/₄ cup thickened cream

1 Grease 2 deep 20cm round cake pans.

2 Beat egg whites in medium bowl with electric mixer until soft peaks form; gradually add sugar, beating until dissolved after additions. Beat in egg yolks and golden syrup.

3 Triple-sift dry ingredients, fold into mixture.

4 Pour mixture into prepared pans. Bake in moderately hot oven about 18 minutes. Turn sponges immediately onto wire racks to cool.

5 Beat cream until soft peaks form, join cakes with cream. Dust top with a little sifted icing sugar, if desired.

recipe best made on day of serving
store covered, in refrigerator
freeze unfilled cake suitable
microwave not suitable

carrot cake

Believed to be of American origin, carrot cakes started to become very popular in the 1950s, and continue as favourites today. The cream cheese frosting adds richness. Use 3 medium carrots for this recipe.

1 cup oil

1¹/₃ cups brown sugar, firmly packed

3 eggs

3 cups coarsely grated carrot

1 cup (120g) chopped walnuts or pecans

¹/₂ cup chopped raisins

2¹/₂ cups self-raising flour

¹/₂ teaspoon bicarbonate of soda

2 teaspoons mixed spice

CREAM CHEESE FROSTING

30g butter

80g packaged cream cheese, softened

1 teaspoon grated lemon rind

1 tablespoon lemon juice

1¹/₂ cups icing sugar

1 Grease 15cm x 25cm loaf pan, line base with paper; grease paper.

2 Beat oil, sugar and eggs in small bowl with electric mixer until thick and creamy.

3 Transfer mixture to large bowl; stir in carrot, nuts and raisins, then sifted dry ingredients.

4 Pour mixture into prepared pan; bake in moderate oven 45 minutes.

5 Cover loosely with foil; bake about further 45 minutes. Stand a few minutes before turning onto wire rack to cool. Top cold cake with cream cheese frosting.

cream cheese frosting Beat butter, cheese, rind and juice in small bowl with electric mixer, beat until light and fluffy; gradually beat in sifted icing sugar.

recipe can be made 2 days ahead

store in airtight container

freeze suitable

microwave not suitable

poppy seed cake

$^1/_3$ cup poppy seeds

$^3/_4$ cup milk

180g butter, softened

2 teaspoons vanilla essence

1 cup caster sugar

3 eggs, lightly beaten

2 cups self-raising flour

1 Grease 14cm x 21cm loaf pan, line base with paper; grease paper.

2 Combine poppy seeds and milk in medium bowl; cover, stand 1 hour.

3 Add butter, essence, sugar, eggs and sifted flour to poppy seed mixture; beat mixture on low speed with electric mixer until combined. Beat on medium speed about 3 minutes or until mixture is slightly changed in colour.

4 Pour mixture into prepared pan; bake in moderate oven about 1 hour. Stand in pan 5 minutes before turning onto wire rack to cool.

recipe can be made a day ahead

store in airtight container

freeze suitable

microwave not suitable

caraway seed cake

180g butter

$^2/_3$ cup caster sugar

3 eggs

1 tablespoon caraway seeds

1$^1/_2$ cups self-raising flour

$^1/_4$ cup milk

1 Grease 14cm x 21cm loaf pan.

2 Beat butter and sugar in small bowl with electric mixer until light and fluffy; beat in eggs, 1 at a time, until combined.

3 Transfer mixture to large bowl; stir in seeds, sifted flour and milk.

4 Spread mixture into prepared pan; bake in moderate oven about 1 hour.

recipe can be made 2 days ahead

store in airtight container

freeze suitable

microwave not suitable

poppy seed cake *(above)*
caraway seed cake *(below)*

streusel coffee cake

Originally from Bohemia, in central Europe, this delicious cake has since been adopted as their own by the cooks of Vienna, Germany and Alsace. The topping, which has a good buttery texture, should be made first.

180g butter
2 teaspoons vanilla essence
1 cup caster sugar
3 eggs
1¹/₂ cups self-raising flour
³/₄ cup plain flour
¹/₂ cup sour cream

TOPPING
³/₄ cup plain flour
3 teaspoons ground cinnamon
60g butter
¹/₃ cup brown sugar

1 Grease 20cm x 30cm lamington pan.

2 Have butter for cake at room temperature. Beat butter, essence and sugar in small bowl, with electric mixer, until light and fluffy; beat in eggs, 1 at a time, until combined.

3 Transfer mixture to large bowl; stir in sifted flours and cream.

4 Spread mixture into prepared pan. Coarsely grate topping over cake; bake in moderate oven about 35 minutes. Stand cake 5 minutes before turning onto wire rack to cool.

topping Sift flour and cinnamon into bowl, rub in butter, stir in sugar. Press mixture into a ball, cover; freeze about 30 minutes or until firm.

recipe can be made 2 days ahead
store in airtight container
freeze suitable
microwave not suitable

madeira cake

This cake does not actually contain madeira. It is a plain cake, always topped with peel, and was served with a glass of madeira in Victorian England.

180g butter, softened

2 teaspoons grated lemon rind

2/3 cup caster sugar

3 eggs

3/4 cup plain flour

3/4 cup self-raising flour

1/3 cup mixed peel

1/4 cup slivered almonds

1 Grease deep 20cm round cake pan, line base with paper; grease paper.

2 Beat butter, rind and sugar in small bowl with electric mixer until light and fluffy; beat in eggs, 1 at a time, until combined.

3 Transfer mixture to large bowl, stir in sifted flours.

4 Spread mixture into prepared pan; bake in moderately slow oven 20 minutes. Sprinkle peel and nuts evenly over cake. Bake about further 40 minutes. Stand cake 5 minutes before turning onto wire rack to cool.

recipe can be made a day ahead

store in airtight container

freeze suitable

microwave not suitable

lumberjack cake

**2 large (400g) apples,
    finely chopped**

1 cup (200g) chopped dates

1 teaspoon bicarbonate of soda

1 cup boiling water

125g butter

1 teaspoon vanilla essence

1 cup sugar

1 egg

1¹/₂ cups plain flour

TOPPING

60g butter

¹/₂ cup brown sugar, firmly packed

¹/₂ cup milk

²/₃ cup shredded coconut

1 Grease deep 19cm square cake pan, line base with paper; grease paper. Combine apples, dates, soda and water in bowl, cover; stand until warm.

2 Beat butter, essence and sugar in small bowl with electric mixer until light and creamy; add egg, beat until combined. Transfer mixture to large bowl, stir in sifted flour alternately with apple mixture; pour into prepared pan.

3 Bake in moderate oven 50 minutes, spread with topping; bake about 30 minutes further, or until topping is golden brown. Cool cake in pan.

topping Combine butter, sugar, milk and coconut in pan, stir over low heat until butter is melted and sugar dissolved.

Recipe can be made a week ahead
storage covered, in refrigerator
freeze suitable
microwave not suitable

swiss roll

Also known as jam roll, or jelly roll in the United States, this has long been a favourite British cake, although its origins seem obscure. It can also be rolled with a cream filling.

3 eggs, separated
1/2 cup caster sugar
3/4 cup self-raising flour
2 tablespoons hot milk
caster sugar, extra
1/2 cup jam, warmed

1 Grease 26cm x 32cm Swiss roll pan, line base and sides with paper; grease paper.

2 Beat egg whites in small bowl with electric mixer until soft peaks form; gradually add sugar, beating until dissolved between additions.

3 Add yolks one at a time, beating well until thick and light. Fold in triple-sifted flour and milk. Pour mixture into prepared pan.

4 Bake in hot oven about 8 minutes.

5 Meanwhile, place a sheet of paper same size as sponge on bench, sprinkle lightly with extra caster sugar. When sponge is cooked, turn immediately onto paper, quickly peel away lining paper. Cut off crisp edge from long sides, spread sponge evenly with jam, commence rolling from short side with help of paper. Lift sponge onto wire rack to cool.

Recipe best made on day of serving
freeze suitable
microwave jam suitable

biscuits and slices

Fresh from the oven, these biscuits and slices are liable to create a family stampede. We've used fruits, nuts, spices, caramel and, of course, chocolate to create a batch of irresistible classics. Whatever your favourite morning or afternoon treat – gingernuts or chocolate brownies, melting moments or anzacs – you'll find the recipe here.

florentines

³/₄ cup sultanas
2 cups (60g) Corn Flakes
³/₄ cup unsalted roasted peanuts, chopped
¹/₂ cup chopped red glacé cherries
²/₃ cup sweetened condensed milk
150g dark chocolate, melted

1 Combine sultanas, Corn Flakes, peanuts, cherries and milk in bowl; mix well.

2 Place 1¹/₂-tablespoon portions of mixture about 5cm apart on oven trays covered with baking paper.

3 Bake in moderate oven about 10 minutes or until lightly browned; cool on trays.

4 Spread base of each biscuit with chocolate. Make wavy lines in chocolate with fork just before chocolate sets.

MAKES ABOUT 18

recipe can be made a month ahead
store covered, in refrigerator
freeze suitable
microwave chocolate suitable

melting chocolate

Choose a heatproof bowl that just fits inside a small saucepan; add enough water to the pan to come almost to the level of the bottom of the bowl, then bring it to a boil. Chop the chocolate roughly, and place it in the bowl over the pan of boiling water. Remove from the heat, and stir constantly until the chocolate is melted.

afghan biscuits

180g butter
¹/₃ cup caster sugar
1¹/₂ cups plain flour
1 tablespoon cocoa
1 cup Corn Flakes, lightly crushed
¹/₄ cup coconut, toasted

CHOCOLATE ICING

³/₄ cup icing sugar
1 tablespoon cocoa
1 teaspoon soft butter
2 tablespoons water,
  approximately

1 Beat butter and sugar in small bowl with electric mixer until light and fluffy. Stir in sifted flour and cocoa, then Corn Flakes and coconut in 2 batches.

2 Place 3-level-teaspoon portions of mixture about 3cm apart on lightly greased oven trays.

3 Bake in moderate oven about 12 minutes or until biscuits are firm and lightly browned. Stand biscuits 5 minutes before lifting onto wire rack to cool.

4 Spread warm chocolate icing quickly onto biscuits.

chocolate icing Combine sifted icing sugar and cocoa in small heatproof bowl; stir in butter and enough water to make a stiff paste. Stir over hot water until spreadable.

MAKES ABOUT 30
recipe can be made a week ahead
store in airtight container
freeze uniced biscuits suitable
microwave not suitable

garibaldi slice

These biscuits were unkindly called "squashed flies" by children, probably due to the appearance and slightly acid flavour of the filling.

¹/₂ cup currants
¹/₂ cup raisins
1¹/₂ cups (240g) sultanas
3 cups plain flour
250g butter, chopped
¹/₃ cup caster sugar
2 egg yolks
2 tablespoons water,
  approximately
caster sugar, extra

1 Grease 26cm x 32cm Swiss roll pan. Blend or process fruit until chopped.

2 Sift flour into bowl, rub in butter, stir in sugar. Add yolks and enough water to mix to a soft dough. Turn dough onto floured surface, knead lightly until smooth; cover, refrigerate 30 minutes.

3 Divide dough in half; roll 1 portion between sheets of greaseproof paper until large enough to fit base of prepared pan. Lift pastry into pan. Spread with fruit. Roll remaining pastry large enough to cover fruit; place over fruit. Press all over with hand to join slice; trim edges.

4 Score into rectangles through top layer of pastry. Brush with a little water, sprinkle with a little extra sugar; prick with fork.

5 Bake in moderately hot oven 10 minutes. Reduce heat to moderate; bake about further 30 minutes or until browned. Cut slice while hot; cool in pan.

recipe can be made a week ahead
store in airtight container
freeze suitable
microwave not suitable

gingernuts

Ginger has long been used as a flavouring for biscuits. These deliciously crisp gingernuts are also known as ginger snaps.

90g butter
1/3 cup brown sugar
1/3 cup golden syrup
11/3 cups plain flour
3/4 teaspoon bicarbonate of soda
1 teaspoon ground cinnamon
1 tablespoon ground ginger
1/4 teaspoon ground cloves

1 Combine butter, sugar and golden syrup in pan; stir over heat until butter is melted. Remove from heat, stir in sifted dry ingredients; stand until mixture feels warm to the touch.

2 Roll 2-level-teaspoon portions of mixture into balls, place about 3cm apart on greased oven trays; flatten slightly.

3 Bake in moderate oven about 12 minutes or until browned. Loosen biscuits; cool on trays.

MAKES ABOUT 35

recipe can be made a week ahead
store in airtight container
freeze suitable
microwave not suitable

chocolate chip cookies

One story suggests that these were created by a housewife in Massachusetts, in the United States, in 1929. They are also known as Toll House Cookies.

90g butter
1 teaspoon vanilla essence
1/3 cup caster sugar
1/3 cup brown sugar
1 egg
1/2 cup self-raising flour
3/4 cup plain flour
3/4 cup Choc Bits
1/2 cup chopped pecans or walnuts
1 tablespoon milk

1 Beat butter, essence and sugars in small bowl with electric mixer until light and fluffy, beat in egg. Stir in flours, Choc Bits, nuts and milk.

2 Drop heaped tablespoons of mixture onto lightly greased oven trays, about 3cm apart.

3 Bake in moderate oven about 12 minutes or until firm and lightly browned. Stand on trays 5 minutes before lifting onto wire racks to cool.

MAKES ABOUT 18
recipe can be made 4 days ahead
store in airtight container
freeze suitable
microwave not suitable

armenian nutmeg cake

Armenian cooking is noted for its use of spices. In this recipe, nutmeg adds fragrance and taste to a not-too-sweet cake that cooks in two layers.

1 cup self-raising flour

1 cup plain flour

1 teaspoon ground nutmeg

125g butter

1¹/₂ cups brown sugar, lightly packed

1 teaspoon bicarbonate of soda

³/₄ cup milk

1 egg, lightly beaten

¹/₂ cup chopped walnuts or pecans

1 Grease 20cm x 30cm lamington pan.

2 Sift flours and nutmeg into large bowl; rub in butter, mix in sugar (or process until crumbly). Press 1¹/₂ cups of this mixture into prepared pan.

3 Stir combined soda and milk into remaining dry ingredients with egg and nuts, mix well; pour into prepared pan.

4 Bake in moderate oven about 35 minutes. Stand 5 minutes before turning onto wire rack to cool.

MAKES ABOUT 35

recipe can be made 2 days ahead

store in airtight container

freeze suitable

microwave not suitable

anzac biscuits

It is thought that anzac biscuits were not named until after World War I, when they were made and sold as fund-raisers for returned solders. It is best to use the traditional (not quick cook) oats in our version.

1 cup rolled oats

1 cup plain flour

1 cup sugar

3/4 cup coconut

125g butter

1 tablespoon golden syrup

1 teaspoon bicarbonate of soda

2 tablespoons boiling water

1 Combine oats, sifted flour, sugar and coconut in large bowl.

2 Combine butter and golden syrup in pan; stir over low heat until butter is melted. Combine soda and water, add to butter mixture; stir into dry ingredients while mixture is warm.

3 Place 3-level-teaspoon portions of mixture about 4cm apart on greased oven trays; press down lightly.

4 Bake in slow oven about 20 minutes or until golden brown. Loosen biscuits while warm, cool on trays.

MAKES ABOUT 30

recipe can be made 4 days ahead

store in airtight container

freeze suitable

microwave not suitable

chocolate brownies

An American creation, brownies are extravagantly rich and luscious, and usually made with lashings of chocolate.

30g butter
250g dark chocolate, finely chopped
80g butter, extra
2 teaspoons vanilla essence
1 cup brown sugar, firmly packed
2 eggs
1/2 cup plain flour
1/2 cup chopped roasted hazelnuts
1/3 cup sour cream

CHOCOLATE ICING

125g dark chocolate, chopped
60g unsalted butter

1 Grease deep 19cm square cake pan, line base with paper; grease paper.

2 Melt butter in pan, add chocolate, stir over low heat until chocolate is melted; cool 5 minutes.

3 Beat extra butter, essence and sugar in small bowl with electric mixer until light and fluffy; beat in eggs 1 at a time. Transfer mixture to large bowl. Stir in sifted flour, then chocolate mixture, nuts and cream.

4 Spread mixture into prepared pan. Bake in moderate oven about 45 minutes; cool in pan.

5 Turn slice from pan, remove paper. Spread slice with chocolate icing; cut when set.

chocolate icing Melt chocolate and butter over simmering water; cool to room temperature. Beat with wooden spoon until thick and spreadable.
recipe can be made 3 days ahead
store in airtight container
freeze suitable
microwave butter and chocolate mixtures suitable

peanut slice

60g butter

2 tablespoons caster sugar

1 egg, lightly beaten

1 cup plain flour

2 tablespoons self-raising flour

1/4 cup raspberry jam

TOPPING

2 eggs, separated

3/4 cup caster sugar

30g butter, melted

1 cup (90g) coconut

1 1/2 cups (250g) chopped roasted unsalted peanuts

1 cup (30g) Corn Flakes

1 Grease 20cm x 30cm lamington pan.

2 Beat butter and sugar in small bowl with electric mixer until creamy; gradually add egg, beat until combined. Stir in sifted flours.

3 Press mixture over base of prepared pan, prick well with fork. Bake in moderately hot oven about 10 minutes or until base is firm; cool.

4 Spread jam over base, spread topping over jam. Bake in moderate oven about 30 minutes or until browned and firm; cool in pan. Refrigerate 1 hour before cutting.

topping Beat egg yolks, sugar and butter in small bowl until thick and creamy; stir in coconut and peanuts. Beat egg whites in small bowl until soft peaks form; fold into nut mixture with Corn Flakes.

recipe can be made 3 days ahead

store in airtight container

freeze suitable

microwave not suitable

melting moments

Melting moments, or yo-yos, have a long history. A recipe for them is
included in Mrs Beeton's Cookery and Household Management.

125g butter

1 teaspoon vanilla essence

2 tablespoons icing sugar

³/₄ cup plain flour

¹/₄ cup cornflour

FILLING

30g butter

¹/₂ teaspoon vanilla essence

¹/₂ cup icing sugar

1 teaspoon milk, approximately

1 Beat butter, essence and sifted icing sugar in small bowl with electric mixer until light and fluffy. Stir in sifted flours.

2 Spoon mixture into piping bag fitted with a 1cm fluted tube. Pipe 3cm rosettes about 3cm apart onto lightly greased oven trays.

3 Bake in moderate oven about 10 minutes or until lightly browned; cool on trays. Join cold biscuits with filling.

filling Beat butter, essence and sifted icing sugar in small bowl until light and fluffy; beat in enough milk to make mixture spreadable.

MAKES ABOUT 20

recipe can be made 2 days ahead

store in airtight container

freeze unfilled biscuits suitable

microwave not suitable

caramel chocolate slice

The caramel filling must be stirred constantly during cooking for perfect results.

1 cup self-raising flour
1 cup (90g) coconut
1 cup brown sugar,
  firmly packed
125g butter, melted

FILLING

400g can sweetened
  condensed milk
30g butter
2 tablespoons golden syrup

TOPPING

125g dark chocolate, chopped
30g butter

1 Lightly grease 20cm x 30cm lamington pan.

2 Combine sifted flour, coconut and sugar in bowl; add butter, stir until combined.

3 Press mixture over base of prepared pan. Bake in moderate oven 15 minutes.

4 Pour hot filling over hot base, return to oven 10 minutes; cool.

5 Spread warm topping over filling, stand at room temperature until set.

filling Combine milk, butter and golden syrup in pan; stir over low heat, without boiling, about 15 minutes or until mixture is golden brown.

topping Combine chocolate and butter in pan; stir over low heat until smooth.

recipe can be made 3 days ahead
store in airtight container
freeze not suitable
microwave topping suitable

caramel corn flake chews

These biscuits do not contain any flour.

125g butter
1/2 cup brown sugar, firmly packed
1/4 cup caster sugar
1/2 cup coconut
3 cups Corn Flakes, lightly crushed
1 egg, lightly beaten
1/2 cup finely chopped mixed nuts

1 Melt butter in large pan, add sugars; cook, stirring, until combined.

2 Remove from heat, stir in coconut, Corn Flakes, egg and nuts; stir gently until combined.

3 Place level tablespoons of mixture about 3cm apart on lightly greased oven trays.

4 Bake in moderate oven about 15 minutes or until golden brown. Stand 5 minutes before removing from trays to cool on wire rack.

MAKES ABOUT 25
recipe can be made a week ahead
store in airtight container
freeze suitable
microwave not suitable

chester squares

The surprise ingredient here is crumbled fruit cake. Believed to be of English origin, chester squares are a delicious way of using up those Christmas leftovers.

90g butter

1/4 cup caster sugar

1 egg

2 tablespoons self-raising flour

1¼ cups plain flour

2 teaspoons caster sugar, extra

FILLING

90g butter

1/3 cup caster sugar

1 egg

2 tablespoons apricot jam

2 cups (about 250g) moist fruit cake crumbs

1/2 cup self-raising flour

2 teaspoons mixed spice

1/2 cup milk

1 Lightly grease 20cm x 30cm lamington pan.

2 Beat butter and sugar in small bowl with electric mixer until just combined; add egg, beat until combined. Fold in sifted flours in 2 batches.

2 Turn dough onto floured surface, knead until smooth. Divide dough in half; cover, refrigerate 30 minutes.

3 Divide pastry in half. Roll 1 portion between sheets of greaseproof paper large enough to fit base of prepared pan; trim edges. Spread filling evenly over pastry base. Roll remaining pastry large enough to cover filling, place over filling; trim edges.

4 Brush pastry with water, sprinkle with extra sugar, prick with fork.

5 Bake in moderate oven about 45 minutes or until golden brown. Stand slice 10 minutes before turning onto wire rack to cool.

filling Beat butter, sugar and egg in small bowl with electric mixer until light and fluffy; stir in jam and crumbs, then sifted flour, spice and milk.

recipe can be made 4 days ahead

store in airtight container

freeze suitable

microwave not suitable

chocolate peppermint slice

1¹/2 cups self-raising flour
¹/2 cup coconut
¹/2 cup brown sugar, firmly packed
125g butter, melted

FILLING

30g Copha
1³/4 cups icing sugar
2 tablespoons milk
¹/2 teaspoon peppermint essence

TOPPING

125g dark chocolate, chopped
30g butter

1 Lightly grease 20cm x 30cm lamington pan, line with paper; grease paper.

2 Combine sifted flour, coconut and sugar in bowl; add butter, stir until combined.

3 Press mixture over base of prepared pan. Bake in moderate oven 20 minutes. Spread base with filling while hot; cool. Spread with topping; refrigerate until set.

filling Melt Copha in pan; stir in sifted icing sugar, milk and essence.

topping Combine chocolate and butter in pan; stir over low heat until smooth.

recipe can be made 3 days ahead
store covered, in refrigerator
freeze not suitable
microwave topping suitable

desserts and pies

Here are recipes for self-indulgence, of the sweetest kind. Lemon delicious, bread and butter pudding, chocolate mousse, apple strudel – these much-loved desserts leave nothing to be desired. Some are quick to prepare, some take more time, but all will provide a memorable finish to a meal.

queen of puddings

Also called Queen Pudding, this dish, based on a 17th century version, was created for Queen Victoria by her chefs at Buckingham Palace.

2 cups (140g) stale breadcrumbs
1 tablespoon caster sugar
2 teaspoons vanilla essence
1 teaspoon grated lemon rind
2¹/2 cups milk
60g butter
4 eggs, separated
¹/4 cup raspberry jam
³/4 cup caster sugar, extra

1 Combine breadcrumbs, caster sugar, essence and rind in large bowl. Heat milk and butter in pan until almost boiling, stir into bread mixture; stand 10 minutes. Stir yolks into bread mixture.

2 Divide mixture into 6 ovenproof dishes (³/4-cup capacity). Bake puddings, uncovered, in moderate oven about 30 minutes or until set.

3 Carefully spread top of puddings with warmed jam.

4 Beat egg whites in small bowl with electric mixer until soft peaks form; gradually add extra caster sugar, beat until sugar is dissolved. Spoon meringue evenly over puddings.

5 Bake puddings in moderate oven about 10 minutes or until lightly coloured.

SERVES 6

recipe best made just before serving
freeze not suitable
microwave not suitable

crepes suzette

Perhaps the most famous fine "pancakes" in the world, crepes Suzette have a fabulous, romantic history involving high society and wonderful dinners.

³/₄ cup plain flour

3 eggs

2 tablespoons oil

³/₄ cup milk

SAUCE

125g butter

¹/₂ cup caster sugar

1¹/₂ cups fresh orange juice, strained

2 tablespoons lemon juice

¹/₃ cup Grand Marnier

1 Sift flour into medium bowl, make well in centre, add eggs and oil; gradually stir in milk, whisk until smooth. Cover; stand 1 hour.

2 Heat greased heavy-based crepe pan. Pour 2 to 3 tablespoons of batter into pan from a jug, turn pan so that batter coats base evenly. Cook slowly, loosening edge with spatula until crepe is lightly browned underneath. Turn crepe, brown, remove from pan; cover to keep warm. Repeat with remaining batter. Fold crepes in half, then in half again.

3 Place crepes in sauce; heat through gently. Serve crepes with sauce, and orange segments and whipped cream, if desired.

sauce Melt butter in pan, add sugar; cook, stirring, until sugar mixture begins to brown. Add juices; cook, stirring, until caramelised sugar is dissolved. Bring to boil; add liqueur, remove from heat, ignite.

SERVES 4

recipe best made just before serving

freeze crepes suitable

microwave not suitable

custard tart

The secret to making a perfect custard tart is to make sure the pastry case is without cracks and joins.

1¼ cups plain flour
¼ cup self-raising flour
¼ cup caster sugar
90g butter
1 egg
2 teaspoons water, approximately
ground nutmeg

CUSTARD

3 eggs, lightly beaten
1 teaspoon vanilla essence
2 tablespoons caster sugar
2 cups milk

1 Sift flours and sugar into bowl, rub in butter. Add egg and enough water to make ingredients cling together. Press dough into a ball; knead on floured surface until smooth. Cover; refrigerate 30 minutes.

2 Roll dough on floured surface until large enough to line 23cm pie plate. Lift pastry into pie plate, gently ease into side of plate; trim edge. Use scraps of pastry to make a double layer of pastry around edge of plate, joining pastry strips with a little water. Trim edge, pinch a frill around edge of pastry.

3 Place pie plate on oven tray, line pastry with paper, fill with dried beans or rice. Bake in moderately hot oven 10 minutes. Remove paper and beans; bake further 10 minutes or until pastry is lightly browned, cool.

4 Pour custard into pastry case; bake in moderate oven 15 minutes. Sprinkle custard evenly with nutmeg; bake further 15 minutes or until custard is just set, cool. Refrigerate until cold.

custard Whisk eggs, essence and sugar in bowl until combined. Heat milk until hot; quickly whisk into egg mixture.

SERVES 6 TO 8

recipe can be made a day ahead
store covered, in refrigerator
freeze not suitable
microwave not suitable

apple sponge

It is important to have the apple mixture as hot as possible before topping with the sponge mixture. The heat from the apples starts the cooking process.

4 large apples (about 800g)
1/4 cup caster sugar
1/4 cup water

SPONGE TOPPING

2 eggs
1/3 cup caster sugar
2 tablespoons cornflour
2 tablespoons plain flour
2 tablespoons self-raising flour

1 Peel, core, quarter and slice apples. Combine in pan with sugar and water, cover; cook about 10 minutes or until apples are tender.

2 Spoon hot apple mixture into deep 14cm round ovenproof dish (6-cup capacity); spread sponge topping over mixture.

3 Bake in moderate oven about 25 minutes.

sponge topping Beat eggs in small bowl with electric mixer about 7 minutes or until thick and creamy. Gradually add sugar, beating until dissolved after additions. Fold in sifted flours.

SERVES 4 TO 6
recipe best made just before serving
freeze not suitable
microwave apples suitable

apple strudel

Usually considered German or Austrian in origin, the strudel is also claimed by Hungary, where it is called retes; it probably came to all these areas from Turkey, as baklava.

5 large apples (about 1kg)

$1/4$ cup water

1 teaspoon grated lemon rind

1 clove

$1/2$ teaspoon ground cinnamon

$1/2$ teaspoon ground nutmeg

2 tablespoons packaged ground almonds

$3/4$ cup walnuts, chopped

$3/4$ cup sultanas

5 sheets fillo pastry

60g butter, melted

2 tablespoons packaged ground almonds, extra

icing sugar

1 Peel, core, quarter and thinly slice apples. Combine in pan with water, rind and clove, cover; cook about 10 minutes or until apples are tender. Discard clove; cool apple mixture.

2 Combine cold apple mixture in bowl with spices, nuts and sultanas.

3 Layer pastry sheets together, brushing each with butter and sprinkling with extra ground almonds. Spread filling to within 2cm from edge of a long side, leaving 5cm at each end. Fold ends in, roll up like a Swiss roll.

4 Place strudel on greased oven tray, brush with butter. Bake in moderate oven about 40 minutes or until lightly browned.

5 Dust strudel with sifted icing sugar before serving. Serve warm or cold with custard or cream.

SERVES 6

recipe can be made a day ahead

store covered, in refrigerator

freeze not suitable

microwave apples suitable

lemon delicious

Originally an English pudding, this dish is sometimes called baked lemon pudding. There are now many variations. Interestingly, the Australian version has had its name shortened, probably as a time-honoured mark of affection.

3 eggs, separated
1/2 cup caster sugar
30g butter, melted
1 cup milk
2 teaspoons grated lemon rind
1/3 cup lemon juice
1/2 cup self-raising flour
1/2 cup caster sugar, extra

1 Beat egg yolks and sugar in small bowl with electric mixer until thick and creamy; transfer to large bowl. Stir in butter, milk, rind, juice and sifted flour.

2 Beat egg whites in small bowl with electric mixer until soft peaks form; add extra sugar gradually, beating until dissolved after additions. Fold into lemon mixture in 2 batches.

3 Pour mixture into lightly greased ovenproof dish (6-cup capacity), or 6 individual dishes (1-cup capacity). Place in baking dish with enough hot water to come halfway up side of dish, or dishes.

4 Bake in moderate oven about 50 minutes (about 30 minutes for individual dishes) or until pudding is set.

SERVES 6

recipe best made just before serving
freeze not suitable
microwave not suitable

chocolate self-saucing pudding

In this recipe, the mixture separates during cooking to form a cake layer over the smooth, creamy sauce.

60g butter
1/2 cup milk
1 teaspoon vanilla essence
3/4 cup caster sugar
1 cup self-raising flour
1 tablespoon cocoa
3/4 cup brown sugar, firmly packed
1 tablespoon cocoa, extra
2 cups boiling water

1 Combine butter and milk in large pan; stir over heat until butter is melted. Remove from heat; stir in essence and caster sugar, then sifted flour and cocoa.

2 Spread mixture into greased ovenproof dish (6-cup capacity). Sift brown sugar and extra cocoa over mixture, then gently pour boiling water over mixture.

3 Bake in moderate oven about 40 minutes.

SERVES 4 TO 6

recipe best made just before serving
freeze not suitable
microwave suitable

bakewell tart

This dish probably had its origins in Elizabethan times, but was made famous by a cook at the Rutland Arms in Bakewell, England, around 200 years ago.

100g butter
2 tablespoons caster sugar
1 egg yolk
1 cup plain flour
**$^1/_2$ cup packaged
   ground almonds**
**$1^1/_2$ tablespoons
   raspberry jam**
2 tablespoons apricot jam

FILLING

125g butter
$^1/_2$ cup caster sugar
2 eggs
**$^3/_4$ cup packaged
   ground almonds**
2 tablespoons rice flour
**$^1/_2$ teaspoon grated
   lemon rind**

LEMON ICING

$^1/_3$ cup icing sugar
2 teaspoons lemon juice

1 Cream butter, sugar and egg yolk in small bowl with electric mixer until combined. Stir in sifted flour and almonds in 2 batches. Knead dough on floured surface until smooth; cover, refrigerate 30 minutes.

2 Roll dough between sheets of greaseproof paper until large enough to line 24cm flan tin. Lift pastry into tin, ease into side; trim edge.

3 Spread base of pastry with raspberry jam; spread filling over jam.

4 Place tart on oven tray; bake in moderately hot oven 25 minutes or until lightly browned.

5 Place apricot jam in small pan; heat, strain. Brush top of hot tart with hot jam; cool. Pipe or drizzle lemon icing over tart.

filling Cream butter and sugar in small bowl with electric mixer until mixture is light and fluffy; beat in eggs 1 at a time. Stir in almonds, rice flour and rind.

lemon icing Sift icing sugar into small bowl, stir in juice; stir until smooth.

SERVES 8

recipe can be made a day ahead
store in airtight container
freeze suitable
microwave jam suitable

black bottom pie

This pie comes from Kentucky in the United States. Its name comes simply from the fact that the base layer of filling is chocolate.

90g butter
1/4 cup caster sugar
1 egg
1 cup plain flour
1/4 cup self-raising flour
1/2 cup thickened cream
30g dark chocolate, grated

FILLING

1 tablespoon gelatine
1/4 cup milk
1/4 cup caster sugar
3 teaspoons cornflour
1 cup milk, extra
3 eggs, separated
60g dark chocolate, melted
1 teaspoon vanilla essence
1/4 cup caster sugar, extra

1 Cream butter and sugar in small bowl with electric mixer until just combined; add egg, beat until just combined. Stir in sifted flours in 2 batches. Turn dough onto floured surface; knead gently until smooth. Cover; refrigerate 30 minutes.

2 Roll pastry on floured surface until large enough to fit 23cm pie plate. Place pastry in plate, trim edge; prick pastry all over with fork.

3 Bake in moderately hot oven about 15 minutes or until browned; cool.

4 Spread chocolate custard into pastry case; refrigerate until firm. Spread vanilla custard into pastry case; refrigerate until firm. Spread whipped cream over custard, then sprinkle with extra chocolate.

filling Sprinkle gelatine over milk in cup. Blend sugar and cornflour with extra milk in pan; stir over heat until mixture boils and thickens, remove from heat. Quickly stir in egg yolks, then gelatine mixture; stir until smooth.

Divide custard into 2 bowls. Stir chocolate into 1 bowl. Cover both bowls; cool to room temperature.

Stir essence into plain custard. Beat egg whites in small bowl with electric mixer until soft peaks form; gradually add extra sugar, beating until dissolved after additions. Fold egg white mixture into vanilla custard in 2 batches.

SERVES 6 TO 8

recipe can be made a day ahead
store covered, in refrigerator
freeze not suitable
microwave chocolate suitable

pancakes

Historians think that pancakes, in the form of grain meal and water cooked on hot stones, were the first recipe ever invented by primitive cooks. Almost every culture's cuisine has a version, from France's crepes to Mexico's tortillas.

2 cups plain flour

4 eggs, lightly beaten

2 cups milk

butter

1/4 cup lemon juice, approximately

2 tablespoons sugar, approximately

1 Sift flour into bowl, gradually add combined eggs and milk; mix, or blend or process, until mixture is smooth. Cover; stand 30 minutes.

2 Lightly grease heated heavy-based pan with butter; pour about 1/4 cup batter evenly into pan. Cook pancake until lightly browned underneath; turn, cook until lightly browned.

3 Keep pancakes warm while cooking remaining batter. Serve pancakes sprinkled with lemon juice and sugar.

MAKES ABOUT 15

recipe best made close to serving

freeze suitable

microwave not suitable

apple crumble

Tender apple chunks make a tempting contrast with a crisp spice and brown sugar topping. Try different combinations, such as stewed apple with rhubarb, apricots or berries.

5 large apples (about 1kg)
¹/₄ cup sugar
¹/₄ cup water

CRUMBLE

³/₄ cup self-raising flour
¹/₂ teaspoon ground cinnamon
80g butter
¹/₂ cup brown sugar, firmly packed

1　Grease ovenproof dish (5-cup capacity). Peel, core and cut apples into eighths.

2　Combine apples, sugar and water in large pan, cover; cook over low heat about 10 minutes or until apples are tender.

3　Drain apples, discard liquid. Spread apples into prepared dish; sprinkle evenly with crumble mixture.

4　Bake in moderate oven about 30 minutes or until golden brown.

crumble Combine sifted flour and cinnamon in bowl, rub in butter. Add sugar; mix well.

SERVES 4 TO 6

recipe can be made 2 hours before serving
store covered, in refrigerator
freeze not suitable
microwave apples suitable

apple pie

Granny Smith apples, with their green skin and crisp, sweet flesh, are ideal for this pie. They were named after Maria Anne Smith, of Sydney, Australia. She cultivated this variety from Tasmanian apple seeds.

1 cup plain flour
¹/₂ cup self-raising flour
¹/₄ cup cornflour
¹/₄ cup custard powder
1 tablespoon caster sugar
100g butter
1 egg, separated
¹/₃ cup water, approximately
1 tablespoon caster sugar, extra

APPLE FILLING

10 medium apples (about 1.5kg)
¹/₂ cup water
2 tablespoons sugar
¹/₄ teaspoon ground cinnamon
1 teaspoon grated lemon rind

1　Sift flours, custard powder and sugar into bowl, rub in butter. Add egg yolk and enough water to make ingredients cling together. Press dough into ball, knead lightly on floured surface until smooth; cover, refrigerate 30 minutes.

2　Divide dough in half; roll 1 portion between sheets of greaseproof paper until large enough to line base and side of 23cm pie plate. Lift pastry into pie plate. Spoon cold apple filling into pastry case; brush edge of pastry with lightly beaten egg white.

3　Roll remaining pastry until large enough to cover filling; place over filling. Press edges together; trim, pinch edges decoratively. Decorate with pastry scraps, if desired. Brush pastry with a little more egg white. Sprinkle with extra sugar.

4　Bake pie in hot oven 20 minutes. Reduce heat to moderate; bake about further 25 minutes or until pastry is well browned.

apple filling Peel, quarter, core and slice apples. Combine apples in large pan with water, cover; simmer about 5 minutes or until apples are tender. Drain apples, discard liquid. Transfer apples to large bowl, gently stir in sugar, cinnamon and rind; cool.

SERVES 6 TO 8

recipe can be made a day ahead
store covered, in refrigerator
freeze not suitable
microwave apples suitable

apple pie *(left)*
apple crumble *(right)*

bread and butter pudding

Serve hot or cold with stewed or canned fruit and cream. Substitute any dried fruit of your choice in this recipe.

6 thin slices white bread
40g butter
3 eggs
1/4 cup caster sugar
2 1/2 cups milk
1 teaspoon vanilla essence
1/2 cup sultanas
ground nutmeg or ground cinnamon

1 Trim crusts from bread, butter each slice; cut into 4 triangles. Arrange 2 rows of triangles, butter-side up, overlapping slightly, along base of shallow ovenproof dish (8-cup capacity). Centre another row of triangles over first 2 rows, with triangles facing in opposite direction to triangles in first layer.

2 Whisk eggs, sugar, milk and essence together in bowl.

3 Pour 1/2 the custard mixture over bread; stand 10 minutes.

4 Whisk remaining custard mixture again, add sultanas; pour into dish. Sprinkle with nutmeg or cinnamon. Stand dish in baking dish, with enough boiling water to come halfway up side of dish.

5 Bake, uncovered, in moderately slow oven about 50 minutes or until custard is set.

SERVES 4 TO 6
recipe can be made a day ahead
store covered, in refrigerator
freeze not suitable
microwave not suitable

lemon chiffon pie

The French word chiffon *is applied to fabrics and foods that are light, soft and silky. It is perfect to describe the texture of this popular dessert.*

**1³/4 cups (180g) plain sweet
biscuit crumbs**

125g butter, melted

FILLING

4 eggs, separated

¹/3 cup caster sugar

3 teaspoons gelatine

2 teaspoons grated lemon rind

¹/3 cup lemon juice

¹/3 cup water

¹/3 cup caster sugar, extra

1 Combine biscuit crumbs and butter in bowl; mix well. Press firmly over base and side of 23cm pie plate; refrigerate 30 minutes or until firm.

2 Spread filling into crumb crust; refrigerate several hours or until set.

filling Combine egg yolks, caster sugar, gelatine, rind, juice and water in heatproof bowl. Stir over simmering water until mixture has thickened slightly. Remove from heat, pour into large bowl, cover; cool to room temperature. Mixture should be set to about the consistency of unbeaten egg white before remaining ingredients are added.

Beat egg whites in small bowl with electric mixer until soft peaks form; add extra sugar gradually, beating until dissolved after additions. Fold whites through lemon mixture in 2 batches.

SERVES 6 TO 8

recipe can be made a day ahead

store covered, in refrigerator

freeze not suitable

microwave not suitable

impossible pie

Everyone loves a quick-mix recipe. This one obligingly sorts itself out in the oven into 3 layers, hence its name.

¹/₂ cup plain flour

1 cup caster sugar

1 cup (90g) coconut

4 eggs, lightly beaten

2 teaspoons vanilla essence

125g butter, melted

2 cups milk

1 Lightly grease straight-sided 24cm pie dish.

2 Sift flour into bowl; stir in remaining ingredients.

3 Pour mixture into prepared pie dish; bake in moderate oven about 45 minutes or until lightly browned and set.

4 Serve warm or cold, with cream or fruit, if desired.

SERVES 6 TO 8

recipe can be made a day ahead

store covered, in refrigerator

freeze not suitable

microwave not suitable

chocolate mousse

*The essence of a mousse is lightness, indicated by its French name,
which means foam or froth. This chocolate version is delicate yet rich.*

**200g dark chocolate,
  chopped**
30g unsalted butter
3 eggs, separated
**300ml carton thickened
  cream, whipped**

1 Place chocolate in heatproof
  bowl, place over pan of
  simmering water; stir chocolate
  until melted, remove from heat.
  Add butter, stir until melted;
  stir in egg yolks 1 at a time.
  Transfer mixture to large bowl,
  cover; cool.

2 Beat egg whites in small bowl
  with electric mixer until soft
  peaks form. Fold the cream
  and egg whites into chocolate
  mixture in 2 batches.

3 Pour into 12 serving dishes
  (1/3-cup capacity); refrigerate
  several hours or overnight.

4 Serve with extra whipped cream
  and chocolate curls, if desired.

SERVES 12

recipe best made a day ahead
store covered, in refrigerator
freeze not suitable
microwave chocolate and butter
suitable

baked apples

Granny Smith and Golden Delicious apples are the best varieties to use for baking.

4 medium apples (about 600g)
50g butter, softened
1/3 cup brown sugar
1/2 cup sultanas
1 teaspoon ground cinnamon

1 Remove cores from apples, cut 1cm from base of each core, push back into base of each apple to act as a plug. Slit skin of each apple around the centre.

2 Beat butter and sugar in small bowl until smooth, stir in sultanas and cinnamon. Fill apple cavities with creamed sugar mixture.

3 Stand apples in greased ovenproof dish. Bake, uncovered, in moderate oven about 45 minutes or until apples are tender; brush occasionally with pan syrup during cooking.

SERVES 4

recipe best made just before serving
freeze not suitable
microwave suitable

baked custard

Don't aerate the custard by whisking the eggs too much. Its texture when cooked should be creamy smooth.

6 eggs
2 teaspoons vanilla essence
1/3 cup caster sugar
1 litre (4 cups) hot milk
ground nutmeg

1 Whisk eggs, essence and sugar together in bowl. Gradually whisk milk into egg mixture, pour into lightly greased ovenproof dish (6-cup capacity), sprinkle with nutmeg.

2 Stand ovenproof dish in baking dish with enough boiling water to come halfway up side of ovenproof dish.

3 Bake, uncovered, in moderate oven about 45 minutes or until custard is firm.

SERVES 6

recipe can be made a day ahead
store covered, in refrigerator
freeze not suitable
microwave not suitable

baked apples *(left)*
baked custard *(right)*

passionfruit flummery

Flummery originated in rural Britain, where it was made with oatmeal or wheat ears soaked in warm water for up to 3 days. Over time, fruit and gelatine (or isinglass, before gelatine was invented) were used instead of grain, turning it into a jelly-like dessert.

1 tablespoon gelatine
1/2 cup caster sugar
2 tablespoons plain flour
3/4 cup water
**1 cup fresh orange
   juice, strained**
2/3 cup passionfruit pulp

1 Combine gelatine, sugar and flour in pan, gradually stir in water. Stir over heat until mixture boils and thickens. Transfer to medium bowl; stir in juice and passionfruit pulp. Refrigerate until mixture starts to set around edge of bowl.

2 Beat mixture with electric mixer for about 10 minutes or until thick and creamy. Pour into 6 serving glasses (3/4-cup capacity); cover, refrigerate until set.

3 Serve with cream and extra passionfruit pulp, if desired.

SERVES 6

recipe can be made a day ahead
store covered, in refrigerator
freeze not suitable
microwave suitable

pecan pie

Pecans are a native American nut; they were introduced to the world through this famous pie.

1 cup plain flour
90g butter
2 tablespoons water,
  approximately

FILLING

3 eggs, lightly beaten
3/4 cup light corn syrup or
  glucose syrup
1 cup brown sugar, firmly packed
30g butter, melted
1¹/4 cups (125g) pecans

1 Sift flour into bowl, rub in butter. Add enough water to make ingredients cling together. Press dough into a ball, knead gently on floured surface until smooth; cover, refrigerate 30 minutes.

2 Roll dough on floured surface until large enough to line 24cm round loose-based flan tin. Lift pastry into tin, gently ease into side; trim edge.

3 Place tin on oven tray, line pastry with paper, fill with dried beans or rice. Bake in moderately hot oven 10 minutes. Remove paper and beans; bake further 10 minutes or until pastry is lightly browned. Cool.

4 Pour filling into pastry case; bake in moderately slow oven 55 minutes or until set. Cool.

filling Combine all ingredients in bowl; mix well.

SERVES 6 TO 8

recipe can be made 2 days ahead
store in airtight container
freeze suitable
microwave suitable

college pudding

Use the jam of your choice in this steamed pudding.

¹/₄ cup jam
125g butter
1 teaspoon vanilla essence
¹/₂ cup caster sugar
2 eggs
2 cups self-raising flour
¹/₂ cup milk

1 Grease aluminium pudding steamer (8-cup capacity). Spoon jam into base of steamer.

2 Beat butter, essence and sugar in small bowl with electric mixer until light and fluffy. Beat in eggs 1 at a time, beat until combined. Transfer mixture to large bowl; stir in sifted flour and milk in 2 batches.

3 Spread mixture into steamer, cover with greased foil, secure with string or lid. Place steamer in large pan with enough boiling water to come halfway up side of steamer; boil, covered, about 1¹/₂ hours or until firm. Replenish water as necessary.

4 Serve with custard, cream or ice-cream.

SERVES 6 TO 8

recipe best made just before serving
freeze not suitable
microwave not suitable

creamed rice

It is important to use full-cream milk in this recipe; cook rice slowly for creamiest results. Serve with fruit of your choice.

1 litre (4 cups) milk
$^2/_3$ cup caster sugar
$^1/_2$ cup short-grain rice
1 teaspoon vanilla essence

1. Combine milk and sugar in medium pan; bring to boil, stirring. Gradually stir rice into boiling milk.

2. Cover pan tightly. Cook over low heat, stirring occasionally, about 1 hour or until rice is tender and most of the liquid is absorbed.

3. Stir in essence. Serve warm or cold.

SERVES 4 TO 6

recipe can be made a day ahead
store covered, in refrigerator
freeze not suitable
microwave suitable

pavlova

Pavlova is said to have been invented by Perth chef Bert Sachse in the 1930s. It was so named because it was considered to be as light as the dancer Anna Pavlova.

4 egg whites
1 cup caster sugar
1 tablespoon cornflour
1 teaspoon white vinegar
300ml carton thickened cream
2 teaspoons vanilla essence
1 tablespoon icing sugar

1 Cover oven tray with baking paper; mark 18cm circle on paper.

2 Beat egg whites in small bowl with electric mixer until soft peaks form; gradually add caster sugar, beating until dissolved after additions. Fold in cornflour and vinegar.

3 Spread meringue inside circle on prepared tray. For best results, do not squash or flatten mixture but shape side up and in towards the centre, like a mound. Make furrows up side of meringue using small spatula, level top.

4 Bake meringue in very slow oven about 1¼ hours or until dry. Turn oven off, leave meringue to cool in oven with door ajar.

5 An hour before serving, beat cream, essence and sifted icing sugar until soft peaks form. Fill meringue with cream mixture, decorate with fruit of your choice.

SERVES 6 TO 8

meringue can be made 4 days ahead
store in airtight container
freeze not suitable
microwave not suitable

spanish cream

This is an adaptation of the Spanish baked custard known as crème caramel. It is correct that the mixture separates.

2 eggs, separated

1/2 cup caster sugar

2 teaspoons vanilla essence

2 cups milk

2 tablespoons gelatine

1/3 cup hot water

1 Whisk egg yolks, sugar and essence in large pan until creamy; whisk in milk. Stir over heat, without boiling, until sugar is dissolved; bring to boil, remove from heat. Sprinkle gelatine over hot water, stir into milk mixture.

2 Beat egg whites in small bowl with electric mixer until firm peaks form. Fold whites into milk mixture in 2 batches.

3 Pour mixture into wetted mould (4-cup capacity), or into 4 individual dishes (1-cup capacity); refrigerate until firm.

SERVES 4

recipe can be made 2 days ahead

store covered, in refrigerator

freeze not suitable

microwave not suitable

key lime pie

The key lime flourishes in Florida, in the United States, where it's used in many dishes. There are many variations of this famous American recipe, but this is our favourite.

1 cup plain flour
2 teaspoons icing sugar
60g butter
2 teaspoons lemon juice
1 tablespoon water,
approximately

FILLING

3/4 cup sweetened
condensed milk
1 cup (200g) ricotta cheese
3 eggs, separated
2 teaspoons grated
lemon rind
1/3 cup lime juice

1 Sift flour and icing sugar into bowl, rub in butter. Stir in lemon juice and enough water to mix to a soft dough. Knead dough gently on floured surface until smooth; cover, refrigerate 30 minutes.

2 Roll dough between sheets of greaseproof paper until large enough to fit 23cm pie plate. Lift pastry into pie plate, ease into side of plate; trim edge.

3 Place pie plate on oven tray, line pastry with paper, fill with dried beans or rice. Bake in moderately hot oven 10 minutes. Remove paper and beans; bake further 7 minutes or until lightly browned. Cool.

4 Pour filling into pastry case; bake in moderate oven about 25 minutes or until filling is set. Cool.

5 Refrigerate pie until cold; dust with sifted icing sugar just before serving.

filling Blend or process milk, cheese, egg yolks, rind and juice until smooth; transfer to large bowl. Beat egg whites in small bowl until soft peaks form, fold into lime mixture in 2 batches.

SERVES 6 TO 8

recipe best made a day ahead
store covered, in refrigerator
freeze not suitable
microwave not suitable

lemon meringue pie

It is believed that the meringue was invented by a Swiss pastry-cook called Gasparini in 1720. It quickly became a favourite of the French court, and Marie Antoinette was apparently so fond of it that she used to make it with her own regal hands!

1¹/₂ cups plain flour

3 teaspoons icing sugar

140g butter

1 egg yolk, lightly beaten

2 tablespoons water, approximately

FILLING

¹/₂ cup cornflour

1 cup caster sugar

¹/₂ cup lemon juice

1¹/₄ cups water

2 teaspoons grated lemon rind

3 egg yolks

60g unsalted butter

MERINGUE

3 egg whites

¹/₂ cup caster sugar

1 Lightly grease 24cm flan tin.

2 Sift flour and icing sugar into bowl, rub in butter. Add yolk and enough water to make ingredients cling together. Press dough into ball, knead gently on floured surface until smooth; cover, refrigerate 30 minutes.

3 Roll dough on floured surface until large enough to line prepared tin. Lift pastry into tin, ease into side; trim edge.

4 Place tin on oven tray, line pastry with paper, fill with dried beans or rice. Bake in moderately hot oven 10 minutes. Remove paper and beans; bake further 10 minutes or until pastry is lightly browned. Cool.

5 Spread filling into pastry case, top with meringue. Bake in moderate oven 5 minutes or until meringue is lightly browned. Stand 5 minutes before serving.

filling Combine cornflour and sugar in pan, gradually stir in juice and water; stir until smooth. Stir over heat until mixture boils and thickens (mixture should be very thick). Reduce heat, simmer, stirring, 30 seconds. Remove from heat, quickly stir in rind, yolks and butter, stir until butter is melted; cover, cool to room temperature.

meringue Beat egg whites in small bowl with electric mixer until soft peaks form; gradually add sugar, beating until dissolved after additions.

SERVES 6 TO 8

recipe can be made a day ahead
store covered, in refrigerator
freeze not suitable
microwave not suitable

rice pudding

This creamy pudding is perhaps the most loved and homely of British desserts.

1/2 cup short-grain rice
21/2 cups milk
1/4 cup caster sugar
2 tablespoons sultanas
1 teaspoon vanilla essence
2 teaspoons butter
ground nutmeg or
  ground cinnamon

1 Lightly grease shallow ovenproof dish (4-cup capacity).

2 Wash rice well under cold water; drain well. Combine rice, milk, sugar, sultanas and essence in prepared dish, mix lightly with a fork. Dot top with butter, sprinkle lightly with nutmeg.

3 Bake in moderately slow oven about 2 hours or until most of the milk has been absorbed.

4 Serve warm or cold with fruit, if desired.

SERVES 4

recipe can be made a day ahead
store covered, in refrigerator
freeze not suitable
microwave not suitable

trifle

*Although now regarded as a good way to use up leftovers,
the trifle was originally a magnificent dish in its own right.*

100g packet strawberry jelly crystals
300g jam sponge roll
1/4 cup sherry
425g can sliced peaches, drained
300ml carton thickened cream, whipped

CUSTARD

2 tablespoons custard powder
2 tablespoons caster sugar
2 cups milk
1 teaspoon vanilla essence

1 Make jelly according to directions on packet; refrigerate until jelly is
just beginning to set.

2 Cut sponge roll into 1cm slices, place over base and around side of
large glass serving bowl; sprinkle with sherry. Pour partly set jelly
over sponge roll; refrigerate until jelly is set.

3 Place peaches over jelly, spread evenly with custard, top with cream;
refrigerate. Serve with fresh fruit, if desired.

custard Blend custard powder and sugar with a little of the milk
in pan, stir in remaining milk. Stir over heat until custard boils and
thickens. Remove from heat, stir in essence; cover, cool.

SERVES 6 TO 8

recipe best made a day ahead
store covered, in refrigerator
freeze not suitable
microwave custard suitable

strawberry shortcake

Although associated with America, the shortcake in fact originated in England and Europe. In England it was known as shortbread, until that name came to be used exclusively for the New Year Scottish shortbreads.

250g butter

1 teaspoon grated lemon rind

1 tablespoon lemon juice

1/2 cup caster sugar

1/3 cup rice flour or ground rice

1 cup self-raising flour

1 1/3 cups plain flour

250g punnet strawberries, halved

1/2 cup strawberry jam

1 Lightly grease 26cm recessed flan tin.

2 Have butter at room temperature. Beat butter, rind, juice and sugar in small bowl with electric mixer until creamy. Stir in sifted flours in 2 batches. Press ingredients together gently, knead lightly until smooth.

3 Press dough evenly into prepared tin. Bake in moderate oven about 20 minutes or until lightly browned; cool in tin.

4 Turn shortcake onto serving plate, decorate with berries. Warm jam in small pan; strain, brush evenly over berries.

shortcake can be made a week ahead; assemble just before serving

store covered, in refrigerator

freeze shortcake suitable

microwave jam suitable

syllabub

*In Elizabethan England, frothing milk was mixed
with wine or cider to create this dish.*

¹/₂ cup dry white wine
2 teaspoons grated lemon rind
2 tablespoons lemon juice
¹/₂ cup caster sugar
300ml carton thickened cream
250g punnet strawberries, sliced

1 Combine wine, rind, juice and sugar in small bowl; stir
until sugar is dissolved. Add cream; beat with electric
mixer until soft peaks form.

2 Divide berries between 6 glasses. Serve syllabub over
berries; refrigerate 2 hours before serving. Serve syllabub
with extra berries and lemon rind, if desired.

SERVES 6

recipe can be made a day ahead
store covered, in refrigerator
freeze not suitable

rum baba

*It is thought that King Leszczynski of Poland invented
the earliest version of this recipe in 1609.*

15g compressed yeast
¹/₄ cup plain flour
¹/₄ cup warm milk
³/₄ cup plain flour, extra
2 tablespoons caster sugar
2 eggs, lightly beaten
60g butter, melted

RUM SYRUP

1¹/₂ cups caster sugar
1 cup water
2 tablespoons dark rum

1 Grease 6 moulds (¹/₂-cup capacity).

2 Cream yeast with flour and milk in small bowl; cover, stand in warm place about 10 minutes or until mixture is frothy.

3 Sift extra flour and sugar into large bowl, stir in yeast mixture, eggs and butter; beat about 3 minutes with wooden spoon until batter is smooth. Place batter in large greased bowl, cover; stand in warm place about 40 minutes or until batter has doubled in size.

4 Beat batter again. Divide batter between prepared moulds; stand, uncovered, until batter rises three-quarters of the way up side of moulds. Place moulds on oven tray; bake in moderately hot oven about 15 minutes. Cover tops if beginning to darken too much.

5 Turn babas onto wire rack over tray, pour hot rum syrup over hot babas. Place babas in serving plates; pour syrup from tray over babas until all syrup has been absorbed.

rum syrup Combine sugar and water in pan; stir over heat, without boiling, until sugar is dissolved. Bring to boil; boil, uncovered, without stirring, 2 minutes. Remove from heat, stir in rum.

MAKES 6

recipe can be made a day ahead
store in airtight container
freeze suitable without syrup
microwave not suitable

snow eggs

Also known as floating islands, this dessert is an adaptation of a French pudding, in which a stale sponge cake, steeped in liqueur, was floated in a bowl of custard.

4 eggs, separated
1 cup caster sugar
2 cups milk
1/3 cup caster sugar, extra
2 teaspoons vanilla essence

CARAMEL TOPPING
1/2 cup sugar
1/4 cup water

1 Beat whites in small bowl with electric mixer until soft peaks form; gradually add sugar, beating until dissolved after additions. Combine milk, extra sugar and essence in shallow pan; stir until sugar is dissolved. Bring to boil, remove from heat.

2 Working quickly, shape egg white mixture into egg shapes using 2 dessertspoons, drop shapes into scalded milk; leave 2 minutes. Turn shapes carefully with fork; leave in milk further 2 minutes.

3 Remove shapes from milk with slotted spoon; drain on tray covered with absorbent paper. Repeat with remaining egg white mixture. Reheat milk to scalding between making each new batch of snow eggs.

4 Strain milk through fine sieve, return milk to pan, whisk in egg yolks. Return to heat; stir over heat, without boiling, until mixture thickens slightly.

5 Pour custard into serving dishes, top with snow eggs, drizzle with caramel topping.

caramel topping Combine sugar and water in pan; stir over heat, without boiling, until sugar is dissolved. Boil, without stirring, until sugar syrup is caramel coloured.

SERVES 4 TO 6

recipe best made just before serving
freeze not suitable
microwave not suitable

pumpkin pie

Perhaps the most well known pumpkin recipe comes from the United States, in the form of this delicious pie. You will need to cook about 350g pumpkin for this recipe.

1 cup plain flour
1/4 cup self-raising flour
2 tablespoons cornflour
2 tablespoons icing sugar
125g butter, chopped
2 tablespoons water, approximately

FILLING
2 eggs
1/4 cup brown sugar
2 tablespoons maple syrup
1 cup cooked mashed pumpkin
2/3 cup evaporated milk
1 teaspoon ground cinnamon
1/2 teaspoon ground nutmeg
pinch ground allspice

1 Sift flours and sugar into bowl, rub in butter. Add enough water to make ingredients cling together. Press dough into a ball, knead gently on floured surface until smooth; cover, refrigerate 30 minutes.

2 Roll dough on floured surface until large enough to line 23cm pie plate. Lift pastry into pie plate, ease into side; trim edge. Use scraps of pastry to make a double edge of pastry; trim and decorate edge.

3 Place pie plate on oven tray, line pastry with paper, fill with dried beans or rice. Bake in moderately hot oven 10 minutes. Remove paper and beans; bake further 10 minutes or until lightly browned, cool.

4 Pour filling into pastry case; bake in moderate oven about 50 minutes or until filling is set, cool. Lightly dust with extra sifted icing sugar, if desired.

filling Beat eggs, sugar and maple syrup in small bowl with electric mixer until thick. Stir in pumpkin, milk and spices.

SERVES 6 TO 8

recipe can be made a day ahead
store covered, in refrigerator
freeze not suitable
microwave not suitable

treacle tart

This hearty and very old English recipe was once a feature of restaurant and cafe menus. Its American cousin is known as molasses pie.

1¹/4 cups plain flour
¹/3 cup custard powder
2 tablespoons icing sugar
125g butter, chopped
2 tablespoons milk, approximately

FILLING

1¹/2 cups (100g) stale breadcrumbs
1 cup treacle
2 teaspoons grated lemon rind

1 Sift flour, custard powder and icing sugar into medium bowl, rub in butter. Add enough milk to make ingredients cling together. Press dough into a ball; knead gently on floured surface until smooth. Cover; refrigerate 30 minutes.

2 Roll ²/3 of dough until large enough to line 22cm flan tin. Lift pastry into tin, gently ease into side; trim edge.

3 Place tin on oven tray, line pastry with paper, fill with dried beans or rice. Bake in moderately hot oven 10 minutes. Remove paper and beans; bake further 10 minutes or until lightly browned, cool.

4 Spread filling into pastry case. Roll remaining pastry into a rectangle on floured surface; cut into 1cm strips. Brush edge of pastry case with a little extra milk. Place pastry strips over filling in lattice pattern; brush pastry with a little more milk.

5 Bake in moderate oven about 25 minutes or until pastry is lightly browned. Cool tart in pan.

6 Sprinkle tart with a little icing sugar before serving. Serve with whipped cream or ice-cream.

filling Combine all ingredients in bowl; mix well.

SERVES 6 TO 8

recipe can be made a day ahead
store covered, in refrigerator
freeze suitable
microwave not suitable

peach melba

This splendid dessert was created in 1892 by the renowned French chef Escoffier, in honour of Dame Nellie Melba, an Australian opera singer.

2 cups water
4 fresh firm peaches
vanilla ice-cream

RASPBERRY SAUCE

200g fresh or frozen
** raspberries**
1 tablespoon icing sugar,
** approximately**

1 Place water in pan, bring to boil, add peaches; simmer 5 minutes. Remove peaches from water, place in bowl of cold water. When peaches are cold, remove skins; cut peaches in half, remove stones.

2 Serve peach halves topped with ice-cream and raspberry sauce.

raspberry sauce Push raspberries through fine strainer; sweeten pulp with sifted icing sugar to taste.

SERVES 4

recipe best made close to serving
freeze not suitable
microwave not suitable

sweet treats

Gem scones or chocolate éclairs, lamingtons or shortbread? We've included them all, so you don't have to choose. And they are just a few of the recipes in this roll call of the best sweet treats ever.

brandy snaps

Make a couple of snaps first to establish a precise cooking time, then proceed with remaining mixture, cooking about 4 snaps on a tray at a time. Once you become confident, you can bake several trays at staggered times.

60g butter
1/3 cup brown sugar
2 tablespoons golden syrup
1/2 teaspoon ground ginger
1/2 cup plain flour
1/2 teaspoon lemon juice

1 Combine butter, sugar, golden syrup and ginger in pan; stir over low heat, without boiling, until butter is melted. Remove from heat, stir in sifted flour and juice.

2 Drop rounded teaspoons of mixture about 6cm apart onto greased oven trays.

3 Bake in moderate oven about 7 minutes or until snaps are bubbling and golden brown; remove from oven.

4 Slide a spatula under each snap, then quickly shape into a cone. Place snaps on wire rack to cool and become firm. Fill with whipped cream just before serving.

MAKES ABOUT 20

recipe best made on day of serving
store unfilled brandy snaps in airtight container
freeze not suitable
microwave not suitable

coconut macaroons

Although almonds were the key ingredient in traditional macaroons,
coconut quickly became an equally popular adaptation.

2 egg whites
1/2 cup caster sugar
1 teaspoon vanilla essence
2 tablespoons plain flour
1 1/2 cups (140g) coconut
6 glacé cherries, quartered

1 Beat egg whites in small bowl with electric mixer until soft
   peaks form. Gradually add sugar, beating until dissolved
   after additions. Stir in essence, sifted flour and coconut in
   2 batches.

2 Line oven trays with baking paper. Drop level tablespoons of
   mixture onto trays about 5cm apart. Place a cherry quarter
   on top of each macaroon.

3 Bake in slow oven about 40 minutes or until lightly
   browned; cool on trays.

MAKES ABOUT 25

recipe can be made a week ahead
store in airtight container
freeze suitable
microwave not suitable

buttermilk scones

3 cups (450g) self-raising
  flour
1/4 teaspoon salt
1 teaspoon icing sugar mixture
60g butter
1 3/4 cups (430ml) buttermilk,
  approximately

1 Grease 23cm square slab cake pan.

2 Sift dry ingredients into large bowl, rub in butter. Stir in enough buttermilk to mix to a soft, sticky dough.

3 Turn dough onto floured surface, knead until smooth. Press dough out to 2cm thickness, cut to 5.5cm rounds.

4 Place rounds in prepared pan; bake in very hot oven about 15 minutes.

MAKES 16

recipe best made just before serving
freeze suitable
microwave not suitable

neenish tarts

1¹/₂ cups plain flour
100g butter
1 egg yolk
2 tablespoons lemon juice, approximately

MOCK CREAM

1¹/₂ tablespoons milk
³/₄ cup sugar
¹/₄ cup water
¹/₂ teaspoon gelatine
1¹/₂ tablespoons water, extra
180g unsalted butter
1 teaspoon vanilla essence

GLACE ICING

1¹/₂ cups icing sugar
2 tablespoons milk
¹/₂ teaspoon vanilla essence
1¹/₂ tablespoons cocoa
1¹/₂ teaspoons milk, extra

1 Grease two 12-hole shallow patty pans.

2 Sift flour into bowl, rub in butter. Stir in yolk and enough juice to make ingredients cling together. Press dough into a ball; knead gently on floured surface until smooth. Cover; refrigerate 30 minutes.

3 Roll dough on floured surface to 3mm thick, cut into 7cm rounds. Place rounds in prepared pans; prick all over with fork.

4 Bake pastry cases in moderate oven about 12 minutes or until golden brown. Lift onto wire racks to cool.

5 Fill pastry cases with mock cream, level tops with spatula. Spread a teaspoon of vanilla icing over half of each tart; allow to set. Cover remaining half of each tart with chocolate icing.

mock cream Combine milk, sugar and water in pan; stir over heat, without boiling, until sugar is dissolved. Sprinkle gelatine over extra water, stir into milk mixture, stir until dissolved; cool.
Beat butter and essence in small bowl with electric mixer until as white as possible, gradually add cold milk mixture; beat until light and fluffy. Mixture will thicken on standing.

glacé icing Sift icing sugar into small bowl, stir in milk and essence; beat until smooth. Divide icing into 2 heatproof bowls. Stir sifted cocoa and extra milk into 1 bowl. Stir both icings over hot water until icing is smooth and spreadable.

MAKES 24
recipe can be made 2 days ahead
store covered, in refrigerator
freeze not suitable
microwave not suitable

fruit mince pies

No traditional Christmas feast would be complete without a batch of these delicious festive treats. Fruit mince is available in jars or you can make your own.

2 cups (300g) plain flour
2 tablespoons packaged ground almonds
180g butter
1 teaspoon grated lemon rind
1/4 cup icing sugar
1 egg yolk
1/4 cup milk, approximately
2 cups (500g) fruit mince
1 egg, lightly beaten
icing sugar

FRUIT MINCE

1 small apple, peeled, cored
1/2 cup sultanas
1/3 cup mixed peel
2 tablespoons glacé cherries, chopped
1/3 cup currants
1/3 cup blanched almonds, chopped
1 cup (200g) brown sugar, firmly packed
1/2 teaspoon grated lemon rind
1 tablespoon lemon juice
1/2 teaspoon grated orange rind
1/2 teaspoon ground cinnamon
1/2 teaspoon mixed spice
1/4 teaspoon ground nutmeg
40g butter, melted
2 tablespoons brandy

1 Lightly grease two 12-hole shallow patty pans.

2 Sift flour into bowl, stir in almonds, rub in butter. Stir in rind and sifted icing sugar. Stir in yolk and enough milk to make ingredients cling together. Knead dough on floured surface until smooth, cover; refrigerate 30 minutes.

3 Roll pastry until 3mm thick. Cut out 7.5cm rounds, place in patty pans. Drop tablespoons of fruit mince into each pastry case.

4 Roll scraps of pastry on floured surface, cut out desired shapes. Brush each pastry shape with egg, place egg-side down on fruit mince.

5 Bake in moderately hot oven about 20 minutes or until lightly browned. Dust with a little sifted icing sugar before serving.

fruit mince Finely chop apple and half the sultanas; combine in bowl with remaining sultanas and remaining ingredients, mix well. Transfer mixture to sterilised jar. Store in refrigerator for at least 3 days before using. Makes about 2 cups fruit mince.

MAKES 24

pies can be made a week ahead
store in airtight container
freeze suitable for 2 months
microwave not suitable

rock cakes

2 cups self-raising flour
¹/₄ teaspoon ground cinnamon
90g butter
¹/₃ cup caster sugar
1 cup (160g) sultanas
2 tablespoons mixed peel
1 egg, lightly beaten
¹/₂ cup milk, approximately
1 tablespoon caster sugar, extra

1 Sift flour and cinnamon into large bowl, rub in butter, stir in sugar and fruit. Stir in egg, then enough milk to give a moist but firm consistency.

2 Place 2-level-tablespoon portions of mixture onto lightly greased oven trays about 5cm apart. Sprinkle cakes with a little extra sugar.

3 Bake in moderately hot oven about 15 minutes or until browned. Loosen cakes; cool on trays.

MAKES ABOUT 18

recipe can be made up to 3 days ahead
store in airtight container
freeze suitable
microwave not suitable

chocolate éclairs

Eclair, meaning lightning or flash of light, is the traditional name for a French choux-pastry cake. Cream puffs are also made from choux pastry. Both can be filled with cream flavoured to suit your taste.

80g butter, chopped
1 cup water
1 cup plain flour
4 eggs, lightly beaten
125g dark chocolate, melted
60g unsalted butter, melted

CHANTILLY CREAM

300ml carton thickened cream, whipped
1 teaspoon vanilla essence
2 tablespoons icing sugar, sifted

1 Combine butter and water in pan, bring to boil. Add sifted flour all at once; stir vigorously over heat until mixture leaves side of pan and forms a smooth ball.

2 Transfer mixture to small bowl of electric mixer; beat in eggs 1 at a time, beating well after additions. Mixture should be glossy.

3 Using piping bag fitted with 1.5cm plain tube, pipe 11cm lengths of pastry, about 3cm apart, onto lightly greased oven trays.

4 Bake in hot oven 10 minutes. Reduce to moderate; bake a further 10 minutes or until pastry is lightly browned and crisp.

5 Cut éclairs in half, remove any soft centre. Return to moderate oven for a few minutes to dry out; cool on wire rack.

6 Dip top half of each éclair in combined chocolate and butter, then join halves with chantilly cream just before serving.

chantilly cream Combine all ingredients in small bowl; cover, refrigerate 30 minutes. Beat cream mixture with electric mixer or rotary beater until thick.

MAKES ABOUT 15

VARIATION

cream puffs

Make pastry as indicated above. Drop 2-tablespoon portions of mixture about 5cm apart onto lightly greased oven trays. Proceed as for éclairs.

Split cold puffs in half, join with chantilly cream just before serving. Dust lightly with a little extra sifted icing sugar.

pastry can be cooked a day ahead

store unfilled éclairs or puffs in airtight container
freeze unfilled éclairs or puffs suitable
microwave not suitable

cheesecakes

Small cheesecakes seem to have originated in England. They had nothing to do with cheese, except that the ingredients for the cake layer included curds, which are akin to cheese.

1 cup plain flour

60g butter

¹/₄ cup caster sugar

1 egg yolk

1 teaspoon water, approximately

2 tablespoons jam, approximately

CAKE MIXTURE

60g butter

1 teaspoon vanilla essence

¹/₃ cup caster sugar

1 egg

³/₄ cup self-raising flour

¹/₄ cup milk

1 Lightly grease two 12-hole shallow patty pans. Sift flour into bowl, rub in butter, stir in sugar. Mix in egg yolk and enough water to make ingredients cling together. Press dough into ball; knead gently on floured surface. Cover; refrigerate 30 minutes.

2 Roll dough on floured surface until 2mm thick. Cut into 6cm rounds; place in prepared pans.

3 Place about ¹/₄ teaspoon jam in each pastry case, top with 3 level teaspoons of cake mixture. Roll pastry scraps, cut into thin strips, twist pastry strips, place on top of cake mixture.

4 Bake cheesecakes in moderate oven about 15 minutes or until lightly browned.

cake mixture Cream butter, essence and sugar in small bowl with electric mixer until light and fluffy; add egg, beat until combined. Stir in sifted flour and milk.

MAKES 24

recipe can be made a day ahead

store in airtight container

freeze suitable

microwave not suitable

butterscotch curls

A rich butterscotch mixture of brown sugar, butter and nuts makes a simple scone dough special. Curls are best eaten hot, split and with butter.

60g butter
$1/3$ cup brown sugar
$1/4$ cup chopped walnuts
3 cups self-raising flour
90g butter, extra
$1^1/4$ cups milk, approximately
$1/3$ cup brown sugar, extra

1 Grease deep 20cm round cake pan. Beat butter and sugar together in small bowl with wooden spoon until just combined, spread over base of prepared pan; sprinkle with nuts.

2 Sift flour into bowl, rub in half the extra butter. Add enough milk to mix to a firm dough. Knead gently on floured surface until smooth. Roll dough to 23cm x 28cm rectangle.

3 Melt remaining extra butter, brush over dough, sprinkle with extra sugar. Roll up as for Swiss roll, from long side. Cut into 10 rounds, place cut-side up in prepared pan.

4 Bake in moderately hot oven about 25 minutes.

MAKES 10

recipe can be prepared 3 hours ahead
store covered, at room temperature
freeze uncooked curls suitable
microwave not suitable

palmiers

These traditional Parisian specialties are named after a palm tree because, when baked, they resemble palm fronds. Palmiers were probably invented as a clever way to make use of puff pastry scraps; quick and easy, they're great for afternoon tea.

375g packet frozen puff pastry, thawed
2 tablespoons caster sugar, approximately

1 Roll pastry on surface sprinkled with sugar into 20cm x 35cm rectangle; trim edges with sharp knife. Sprinkle pastry lightly with a little more sugar. Fold in long sides of rectangle so that they meet in the centre, sprinkle with a little more sugar, fold in half lengthways, press lightly; cover, refrigerate 30 minutes.

2 Cut pastry roll into 12mm slices; place slices about 10cm apart on lightly greased oven trays.

3 Bake in moderately hot oven 10 minutes. Turn palmiers with eggslice; bake about further 10 minutes or until crisp. Lift onto wire racks to cool. Lightly dust with sifted icing sugar, if desired.

MAKES ABOUT 25

recipe can be made 2 days ahead
store in airtight container
freeze uncooked suitable
microwave not suitable

palmier variations

Palmiers can be drizzled with melted dark or white chocolate or a thin glacé icing. To make the icing, stir about 1 tablespoon of milk into 1 cup of icing sugar mixture; tint with a few drops of food colouring, if desired. Drizzle the melted chocolate or the icing over hot palmiers so that it sets upon cooling.

chelsea buns

When the London suburb of Chelsea was a village in the country, fashionable people, even royalty, would gather at the Chelsea Bun House to enjoy its delicious fare.

2 x 7g sachets granulated yeast
1 teaspoon caster sugar
1 teaspoon plain flour
1 1/2 cups warm milk
2 cups (280g) currants
1 teaspoon grated lemon rind
1 teaspoon ground cinnamon
1 egg, lightly beaten
4 cups plain flour, extra
125g butter, melted
2/3 cup brown sugar, firmly packed
1 tablespoon caster sugar, extra

ICING

1 cup icing sugar
1 tablespoon milk, approximately
pink food colouring

1 Grease deep 23cm square cake pan.

2 Combine yeast, caster sugar, flour and milk in bowl; cover, stand in warm place about 10 minutes or until mixture is frothy.

3 Place currants in pan, cover with water, bring to boil; remove from heat, cover, cool. Drain currants well; combine in small bowl with rind and cinnamon.

4 Whisk egg into yeast mixture. Sift extra flour into large bowl, stir in yeast mixture, cover; stand in warm place about 40 minutes or until dough has doubled in size.

5 Turn dough onto floured surface, knead 3 minutes or until smooth. Roll dough into 30cm x 40cm rectangle. Brush with one-quarter of the butter, sprinkle with one-third of the brown sugar.

6 Fold one end of the dough to come two-thirds of the way up the dough, fold over top third to cover first fold. Turn dough halfway around to have open ends facing you.

7 Roll dough into 30cm x 40cm rectangle. Repeat folding as before, using same amount of butter and brown sugar. Turn dough halfway round, roll to 30cm x 40cm rectangle. Brush dough with half the remaining butter, sprinkle with remaining brown sugar and the currant mixture.

8 Roll dough firmly from long side like a Swiss roll. Cut dough evenly into nine pieces; place buns, cut-side up, in prepared pan, sprinkle with extra caster sugar. Stand, uncovered, in warm place about 20 minutes or until buns have risen slightly.

9 Drizzle buns with remaining butter; bake in moderately hot oven 5 minutes. Reduce heat to moderate; bake further 25 minutes or until buns are golden brown. Turn buns onto wire rack, drizzle a little icing onto each bun; cool.

icing Sift icing sugar into bowl, stir in enough milk to form a thin, smooth paste; tint with pink colouring.

MAKES 9

recipe can be made 4 hours ahead
store in airtight container
freeze suitable
microwave not suitable

lamingtons

The cake is easier to handle if it's a little stale; day-old cake is ideal. Sponge or butter cake can also be used. Fill lamingtons with jam and cream, if desired.

6 eggs
²/₃ cup caster sugar
¹/₃ cup cornflour
¹/₂ cup plain flour
¹/₃ cup self-raising flour
2 cups (180g) coconut, approximately

ICING

4 cups (500g) icing sugar
¹/₂ cup cocoa
15g butter, melted
²/₃ cup milk

1 Grease 23cm square slab pan. Beat eggs in medium bowl with electric mixer about 10 minutes or until thick and creamy. Gradually beat in sugar, dissolving after additions. Fold in triple-sifted flours.

2 Spread mixture into prepared pan; bake in moderate oven about 30 minutes. Turn cake onto wire rack to cool.

3 Cut cake into 16 squares, dip squares in icing, drain off excess icing, toss squares in coconut. Place lamingtons on wire rack to set.

icing Sift icing sugar and cocoa into heatproof bowl; stir in butter and milk. Stir icing over pan of simmering water until it is of a coating consistency.

MAKES 16
cake best made a day ahead
store in airtight container
freeze suitable
microwave not suitable

pikelets

Use an electric frypan, a frying pan or a solid plate over a griller for cooking pikelets. Turn pikelets just before the bubbles burst for best results.

1 cup self-raising flour
¹/₄ cup caster sugar
pinch bicarbonate of soda
1 egg, lightly beaten
³/₄ cup milk, approximately

1 Sift dry ingredients into medium bowl. Make well in centre; gradually stir in egg and enough milk to give a smooth, creamy pouring consistency.

2 Drop dessertspoons of batter from tip of spoon into heated greased frying pan; allow room for spreading. When bubbles begin to appear, turn pikelets; cook until lightly browned on other side. Serve warm with butter or cream and jam.

MAKES ABOUT 15

recipe best made just before serving
freeze suitable
microwave not suitable

eccles cakes

It is thought the Crusaders introduced these to England when they returned from the Holy Land in the 13th century.

3 sheets ready-rolled puff pastry
1 egg yolk, lightly beaten
caster sugar

FILLING

30g butter
³/₄ cup currants
¹/₄ cup chopped mixed peel
2 tablespoons caster sugar
¹/₂ teaspoon ground nutmeg
¹/₂ teaspoon mixed spice

1 Cut pastry into 11cm rounds. Place a level tablespoon of filling in centre of each round. Pinch edges together to enclose filling. Turn smooth-side up onto floured surface, flatten gently with rolling pin so that currants just show through pastry.

2 Shape into ovals, place on greased oven trays. Brush ovals with egg yolk, sprinkle lightly with sugar, cut 3 small slits in top of each oval.

3 Bake cakes in moderately hot oven about 15 minutes or until browned.

filling Combine butter, fruit, sugar and spices in pan, stir over low heat until butter is melted; cool.

MAKES 12

recipe can be made 2 days ahead
store in airtight container
freeze suitable
microwave filling suitable

cream horns

The pastry shapes are quickly made by wrapping strips around cream horn tins. You can vary the jam you use, and flavour the cream with liqueur or spirits to complement your chosen jam.

**375g packet frozen
    puff pastry, thawed**
milk
¹/₂ cup jam

CHANTILLY CREAM

1 tablespoon icing sugar
1 teaspoon vanilla essence
300ml carton thickened cream

1 Lightly grease eight 5cm x 15cm cream horn tins.

2 Roll pastry thinly on floured surface into a rectangle; cut into 2cm strips. Moisten 1 edge of each strip with water.

3 Starting at point of cone, wind strips around cone, overlapping the moistened edge; do not stretch pastry. Join edge of strips with a little water. Bring pastry to about 1cm from end of cone. Repeat with remaining pastry.

4 Place cones about 3cm apart on lightly greased oven tray, brush pastry lightly and evenly with milk. Bake in moderate oven 30 minutes. Slip tins from pastry horns; bake about further 5 minutes or until pastry is crisp. Cool on wire rack.

5 Spoon jam into pastry horns, spoon or pipe chantilly cream into horns just before serving. Dust with a little icing sugar, if desired.

chantilly cream Combine all ingredients in bowl; refrigerate 30 minutes. Beat with electric mixer or rotary beater until soft peaks form.

MAKES 8

pastry horns can be made a day ahead
store unfilled pastry horns in airtight container
freeze unfilled pastry horns suitable
microwave not suitable

gem scones

Old-fashioned cast gem irons are available from specialty cookware shops, or even second-hand shops.

40g butter
1/3 cup caster sugar
1 egg, lightly beaten
1¹/2 cups self-raising flour
1 cup milk

1 Place 2 ungreased 12-hole gem irons into hot oven.

2 Beat butter and sugar in small bowl with electric mixer until light and fluffy; add egg gradually, beat until combined. Stir in sifted flour and milk in 2 batches.

3 Lightly grease hot gem irons; drop 1 level tablespoon of mixture into each hole.

4 Bake in hot oven about 10 minutes or until lightly browned. Serve scones hot with butter or jam and cream.

MAKES ABOUT 24

recipe best made just before serving
freeze suitable
microwave not suitable

kisses

Various one-bite delicacies are now described as kisses. The name could derive from the days when bread was home-baked, and curly bits of crust, known as "kissing crusts", were broken off the cooling bread and eaten by children.

125g butter
$1/2$ cup caster sugar
1 egg
$1/3$ cup plain flour
$1/4$ cup self-raising flour
$2/3$ cup cornflour
$1/4$ cup custard powder

VIENNA CREAM

60g butter
$3/4$ cup icing sugar
2 teaspoons milk

1   Beat butter and sugar in small bowl with electric mixer until smooth and creamy; add egg, beat only until combined. Stir in sifted dry ingredients in 2 batches.

2   Spoon mixture into piping bag fitted with 1cm tube. Pipe 3cm-diameter rounds of mixture, about 3cm apart, onto lightly greased oven trays.

3   Bake in moderately hot oven about 10 minutes or until lightly browned. Loosen biscuits, cool on trays.

4   Sandwich cold biscuits with Vienna cream; dust with a little extra sifted icing sugar, if desired.

vienna cream   Beat butter until as white as possible. Gradually beat in $1/2$ the sifted icing sugar, then milk; gradually beat in remaining icing sugar.

MAKES ABOUT 40

recipe can be made 3 days ahead
store   in airtight container
freeze   unfilled kisses suitable
microwave   not suitable

1. Grease 30 shallow patty pan holes.

2. Beat butter, essence and sugar in small bowl with electric mixer until smooth and creamy; add egg, beat until just combined. Stir in sifted flour. Turn mixture onto floured surface, knead gently until smooth; cover, refrigerate 30 minutes.

3. Roll pastry on floured surface until 2mm thick, cut 6.5cm rounds from pastry, place in prepared pans.

4. To make stalks, roll pastry scraps to 8mm-diameter sausage; cut 30 x 1.5cm-long stalks. Place on lightly greased oven tray.

5. Bake cases and stalks in moderately hot oven about 12 minutes or until lightly browned. Flatten pastry cases with back of spoon halfway through cooking to remove air bubbles. Cool on wire racks.

6. Spread inside of each pastry case with about 1/2 teaspoon jam, sprinkle with about 1/2 teaspoon nuts. Spread about 2 level teaspoons filling into each case, sprinkle with a little sifted cocoa. Press stalks into filling.

filling Have butter and milk at room temperature. Beat butter, essence and sugar in small bowl with electric mixer until as white as possible. Gradually beat in milk and water a teaspoon at a time.

MAKES ABOUT 30

pastry cases can be prepared 2 days ahead
store in airtight container
freeze pastry cases suitable
microwave not suitable

mushrooms

It is important to have the milk and butter at room temperature when making the butter cream filling.

90g butter
1 teaspoon vanilla essence
1/3 cup caster sugar
1 egg
1²/3 cups plain flour
1/3 cup raspberry jam, approximately
1/3 cup crushed mixed nuts, approximately
2 teaspoons cocoa, approximately

FILLING

90g butter
1/2 teaspoon vanilla essence
1/3 cup caster sugar
1/3 cup milk
1/3 cup water

coconut ice

One of Australia's favourite sweets, this creamy favourite is quick and easy, and needs no cooking.

**5¹/₄ cups (760g) icing
 sugar mixture**
2¹/₂ cups (225g) coconut
**400g can sweetened
 condensed milk**
1 egg white, lightly beaten
pink food colouring

1 Line deep 19cm square cake pan
 with foil.

2 Sift icing sugar into large
 bowl, stir in coconut, then
 milk and egg white; stir until
 well combined.

3 Press half the mixture into
 prepared pan. Tint remaining
 mixture pink, press evenly over
 first layer; cover, refrigerate
 several hours before cutting.
 recipe can be made a week ahead
 store covered, in refrigerator
 freeze not suitable

pumpkin scones

Whatever the impact of her political career, Flo Bjelke-Petersen will long be remembered in Australia for her championing of the pumpkin scone. You will need to cook about 250g pumpkin for this recipe.

40g butter

¹/₄ cup caster sugar

1 egg, lightly beaten

³/₄ cup cooked mashed pumpkin

2¹/₂ cups self-raising flour

¹/₂ teaspoon ground nutmeg

¹/₃ cup milk, approximately

1 Lightly grease two 20cm round sandwich pans.

2 Beat butter and sugar in small bowl with electric mixer until light and fluffy; gradually beat in egg. Transfer mixture to large bowl.

3 Stir in pumpkin, then sifted dry ingredients and enough milk to make a soft sticky dough. Turn dough onto floured surface, knead lightly until smooth.

4 Press dough out to about 2cm in thickness, cut 5cm rounds from dough. Place rounds, just touching, in prepared pans. Brush tops with a little milk.

5 Bake scones in very hot oven about 15 minutes.

MAKES ABOUT 16

recipe best made just before serving

freeze suitable

microwave not suitable

scottish shortbread

Originally another Hogmanay specialty of Scotland, where it originated up to 400 years ago, shortbread has become very popular in many parts of the globe and is now eaten all year.

250g butter

$1/3$ cup caster sugar

2 cups plain flour

$1/2$ cup rice flour or ground rice

1 Have butter at room temperature. Beat butter and sugar in small bowl with electric mixer until combined. Add large spoonfuls of sifted flours to butter mixture, beating after each addition.

2 Press ingredients together gently, knead on floured surface until smooth.

3 Divide dough into 2 portions; shape portions into 18cm rounds. Place rounds on greased oven trays; mark into wedges, prick with fork. Pinch a decorative edge with floured fingers.

4 Bake in slow oven about 30 minutes. Stand 10 minutes before transferring to wire rack to cool. Cut when cold.

MAKES 2

recipe can be made a month ahead
store in airtight container
freeze suitable
microwave not suitable

waffles with caramel sauce

Waffles were eaten in France and Germany more than 500 years ago. Their name derives from the German word wabe, or "honeycomb", which the surface of a waffle resembles.

1³/₄ cups plain flour
¹/₄ cup self-raising flour
¹/₄ cup caster sugar
2 eggs, separated
1¹/₂ cups milk
60g butter, melted
2 tablespoons water

CARAMEL SAUCE

125g butter
1 cup (200g) brown sugar, firmly packed
300ml carton thickened cream

1 Sift flours and sugar into bowl. Make well in centre, gradually stir in combined egg yolks and milk, then butter and water; stir until smooth.

2 Beat egg whites in small bowl until soft peaks form; fold into mixture in 2 batches.

3 Drop about ¹/₃ cup mixture onto prepared waffle iron. Close iron; cook about 2 minutes or until waffle is golden brown. Repeat with remaining mixture.

4 Serve waffles immediately with caramel sauce.

caramel sauce Melt butter in medium pan, add sugar; stir over heat, without boiling, until sugar is dissolved. Bring to boil; simmer, without stirring, 2 minutes. Remove from heat, allow bubbles to subside, stir in cream.

MAKES 12 WAFFLES, 1¹/₂ CUPS SAUCE

sauce can be made a day ahead;
waffles best made just before serving
store sauce, covered, in refrigerator
freeze not suitable
microwave not suitable

vanilla ice-cream

Iced concoctions have a long history, with the Romans enjoying an early version consisting of flavoured snow. Use a shallow pan for freezing the ice-cream in this recipe.

³/₄ cup caster sugar
4cm piece vanilla bean, split
3 x 300ml cartons thickened cream

1 Line a lamington pan with plastic wrap, leave wrap overhanging edges. This makes it easier to remove the ice-cream for beating.

2 Combine sugar, vanilla bean and 1 carton of the cream in pan; stir over heat, without boiling, until sugar is dissolved. Remove from heat, stir in remaining cream; remove vanilla bean.

3 Strain mixture through fine cloth into prepared pan, cover; freeze 3 hours or until just firm.

4 Spoon mixture into large bowl; beat with electric mixer until smooth and creamy. Return to lined pan, cover; freeze 3 hours or until just firm.

5 Repeat beating once more, return to pan, cover; freeze 3 hours or overnight.

MAKES ABOUT 1 LITRE

recipe can be made a week ahead
store covered, in freezer
microwave cream mixture suitable

rocky road

5 teaspoons gelatine

1/2 cup water

1 cup caster sugar

1/3 cup water, extra

2 teaspoons lemon juice

1 teaspoon vanilla essence

pink food colouring

1/3 cup coconut

375g milk chocolate, chopped

30g Copha, chopped

1/2 cup red glacé cherries

1/2 cup unsalted roasted peanuts

1 Grease two 26cm bar pans.

2 Sprinkle gelatine over water in small bowl. Combine sugar and extra water in medium pan; stir over heat, without boiling, until sugar is dissolved. Stir in gelatine mixture, bring to the boil; boil, without stirring, 8 minutes. Remove from heat, stir in juice and essence. Divide mixture into 2 small bowls; cool.

3 Tint 1 bowl of mixture pink. Beat each mixture with electric mixer until thick and holding its own shape. Spread mixtures into prepared pans, refrigerate about 1 hour or until set.

4 Sprinkle coconut over board, turn marshmallow from pans onto board, toss in coconut. Using a hot knife, cut marshmallow into squares.

5 Lightly grease 20cm x 30cm lamington pan, line with strip of foil to cover base and extend over 2 opposite ends.

6 Combine chocolate and Copha in heatproof bowl; stir over pan of simmering water until smooth. Remove from heat, stand 10 minutes.

7 Thinly spread 1/4 cup of chocolate mixture over base of prepared pan. Place marshmallows and remaining coconut in pan, sprinkle with cherries and peanuts. Drizzle remaining chocolate evenly over mixture in pan. Refrigerate until set before cutting.

recipe can be made a week ahead
store covered, in refrigerator
freeze not suitable
microwave not suitable

rum balls

4 cups (400g) fine cake crumbs
¹/4 cup cocoa
¹/4 cup apricot jam, warmed
2 tablespoons dark rum
2 tablespoons water
²/3 cup chocolate sprinkles

1 Combine crumbs and sifted cocoa in bowl; stir in combined strained jam, rum and water.

2 Roll 2 level teaspoons of mixture into balls. Roll balls in chocolate sprinkles. Refrigerate 2 hours before serving.

MAKES ABOUT 45

recipe can be made a week ahead
store covered, in refrigerator
freeze not suitable

hot cross buns

Although these delicious Easter treats are now served on Good Friday, in olden times they were thought to have holy powers and were present in many religious observances.

2 x 7g sachets granulated yeast
1/4 cup caster sugar
11/2 cups warm milk
4 cups plain flour
1 teaspoon mixed spice
1/2 teaspoon ground cinnamon
60g butter
1 egg
3/4 cup sultanas

FLOUR PASTE FOR CROSSES

1/2 cup plain flour
2 teaspoons caster sugar
1/3 cup water, approximately

GLAZE

1 tablespoon caster sugar
1 teaspoon gelatine
1 tablespoon water

1 Combine yeast, sugar and milk in small bowl; cover, stand in warm place about 10 minutes or until mixture is frothy.

2 Sift flour and spices into large bowl, rub in butter. Stir in yeast mixture, egg and sultanas; mix to a soft sticky dough. Cover; stand in warm place about 45 minutes or until dough has doubled in size.

3 Turn dough onto floured surface, knead about 5 minutes or until smooth. Divide dough into 16 pieces, knead into balls. Place balls in greased 23cm square slab pan; cover, stand in warm place about 10 minutes or until buns have risen to top of pan.

4 Place flour paste for crosses in piping bag fitted with small plain tube, pipe crosses on buns.

5 Bake buns in hot oven about 20 minutes or until well browned. Turn buns onto wire rack, brush tops with hot glaze; cool on wire rack.

flour paste for crosses Combine flour and sugar in bowl. Gradually blend in enough water to form a smooth paste.

glaze Combine all ingredients in pan; stir over heat, without boiling, until sugar and gelatine are dissolved.

MAKES 16

recipe can be made a day ahead
store in airtight container
freeze uncooked buns suitable
microwave glaze suitable

cake pans

If using pans that have a non-stick coating, are anodised or are made from stainless steel or tin, best results will be obtained by reducing the oven temperature by 10°C (25°F).

Specialty cake pans
a. 5cm x 15cm cream horn tins
b. 8cm x 17cm nut roll tin
c. 20cm spring form tin
d. 24cm flan tin

Long cake pans
a. 26cm bar pan
b. 20cm x 30cm lamington pan
c. 26cm x 32cm swiss roll pan
d. oven tray

Round cake pans
a. 20cm round sandwich pan
b. 20cm ring cake pan
c. 20cm deep round cake pan

Small cake pans
a. 12-hole gem iron
b. 12-hole shallow patty pan
c. 12-hole deep patty (muffin) pan

Square cake pans
a. 19cm deep square cake pan
b. 23cm square slab pan
c. 23cm deep square cake pan

glossary

Alcohol optional, but gives a special flavour. If desired, substitute fruit juice or water to make up the liquid content of our recipes.

Allspice also known as pimento; tastes like a blend of cinnamon, clove and nutmeg.

Almonds
FLAKED sliced almonds.
GROUND we use packaged commercially ground nuts, unless otherwise specified.
SLIVERED almonds cut lengthwise.

Arrowroot used mostly for thickening; cornflour can be substituted.

Baking powder a raising agent consisting mainly of 2 parts cream of tartar to 1 part bicarbonate of soda (baking soda).

Bicarbonate of soda also known as baking soda.

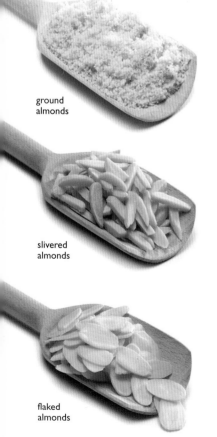

ground almonds

slivered almonds

flaked almonds

Biscuit crumbs, sweet use any plain, sweet biscuits (cookies). Blend or process biscuits until finely and evenly crushed.

Breadcrumbs
PACKAGED fine-textured, purchased white breadcrumbs.
STALE 1- or 2-day-old white bread made into crumbs by blending or processing.

Butter use salted or unsalted (also called sweet) butter; 125g is equal to 1 stick butter.

Buttermilk low-fat milk cultured with bacteria to give a slightly sour, tangy taste; low-fat yogurt can be substituted.

Cachous small, round cake-decorating sweets available in silver, gold or other colours.

Cheese
CREAM also known as "Philadelphia" or "Philly"; a soft milk cheese having no less than 33% butterfat.
RICOTTA a fresh, unripened cheese made from whey.

Chestnut spread made from sweetened, flavoured, pureed chestnuts; available from delicatessens and some supermarkets.

Choc Bits also known as chocolate chips and chocolate morsels; small buds of dark chocolate, made of cocoa liquor, cocoa butter, sugar and an emulsifier, that hold their shape in baking.

Chocolate, dark we used a good-quality cooking chocolate.

Cocoa cocoa powder.

Coconut we used desiccated coconut unless otherwise specified.
ESSENCE extract.
FLAKED flaked and dried coconut flesh.
SHREDDED thin strips of dried coconut flesh.

Copha a solid white shortening based on coconut oil. Kremelta and Palmin can be substituted.

Corn Flakes crisp flakes

demerara sugar

brown sugar

caster sugar

icing sugar mixture

made from toasted corn; a popular breakfast cereal.

Corn syrup available in light or dark colours. Glucose syrup can be substituted.

Cornflour also known as cornstarch; used as a thickening agent.

Cornmeal ground, dried corn (maize); similar to polenta but slightly coarser. One can be substituted for the other but textures will vary.

Cream
FRESH also known as pure cream and pouring cream; has no additives like commercially thickened cream (minimum fat content 35%).
SOUR a thick, commercially cultured soured cream (minimum fat content 35%).
SOUR LIGHT a less dense, commercially cultured soured cream; do not use this instead of sour cream.
THICKENED a whipping cream (minimum fat content 35%) containing a thickener such as gelatine.

Custard powder packaged vanilla pudding mix.

Essence also known as extract. Usually the by-product of distillation of plants.

Flour
RICE flour made from rice; ground rice can be substituted.
PLAIN all-purpose flour, made

flaked coconut

desiccated coconut

shredded coconut

from wheat.

SELF-RAISING substitute plain flour and baking powder in the proportion of 3/4 cup of plain flour to 2 teaspoons of baking powder; sift together several times before using. If using an 8oz measuring cup, use 1 cup of plain flour to 2 teaspoons of baking powder.

Fruit mince also known as mincemeat.

Gelatine we used powdered gelatine.

Ginger

GLACE fresh ginger root preserved in sugar syrup. Crystallised ginger can be substituted if rinsed with warm water and dried well before using.

GROUND also known as powdered ginger; cannot be substituted for fresh ginger.

Glucose syrup (liquid glucose) clear syrup with a consistency like honey; it is made from wheat starch. Available at health food stores and supermarkets. Do not confuse it with the powdered glucose drink.

Golden syrup a by-product of refined sugarcane; pure maple syrup or honey can be substituted.

Grand Marnier an orange-flavoured liqueur.

Greaseproof paper we used this paper to line cake pans etc; do not confuse with the shiny wax paper. It is best to grease greaseproof paper after lining the pan. Baking paper can also be used for lining pans.

Ground rice rice flour can be substituted, although it will give a finer texture than ground rice.

Hazelnuts, ground we used packaged commercially ground nuts.

Hundreds and thousands nonpareils.

Jam also known as preserves or conserve; most often made from fruit.

Jelly crystals fruit-flavoured

gelatine crystals available from supermarkets.

Kirsch a cherry-flavoured liqueur.

Lemon butter lemon cheese or lemon curd.

Liqueurs we have used a variety of liqueurs; if desired, you can use brandy instead (but the flavour will change). If alcohol is not desirable, substitute fruit juice of an equivalent flavour or milk or water to balance the liquid proportions in the recipe.

Madeira wine fortified with brandy.

Maple syrup distilled sap of the maple tree.

Marsala a sweet fortified wine.

Marzipan, roll a smooth, firm confectionery paste.

Milk we used full-cream homogenised milk unless otherwise specified.

EVAPORATED unsweetened canned milk from which water has been extracted.

SWEETENED CONDENSED a canned milk product consisting of milk with more than half the water content removed and sugar added to the milk that remains.

Mixed dried fruit a combination of sultanas, raisins, currants, mixed peel and cherries.

Mixed peel a mixture of crystallised citrus peel; also known as candied peel.

Mixed spice a blend of ground spices, usually consisting of cinnamon, allspice and nutmeg.

Oil we used polyunsaturated vegetable oil unless otherwise specified.

Puff pastry, ready-rolled frozen sheets of puff pastry available from supermarkets.

Punnet small basket usually holding about 250g fruit.

Rice Bubbles rice crispies.

Rind zest.

Rolled oats whole oat

ground ginger

glacé ginger

grains that are steamed and flattened, then dried and packaged for consumption as cereal product.

Rum, dark we used an underproof (not overproof) rum for a more subtle flavour.

Sago also sold as seed tapioca. Tapioca can be used as a substitute for sago; it will need more cooking.

Sugar we used coarse granulated table sugar (also known as crystal sugar) unless otherwise specified.

BROWN an extremely soft finely granulated sugar retaining molasses for its deep colour and flavour.

CASTER also known as superfine or finely granulated table sugar.

DEMERARA small golden-coloured crystal sugar.

ICING also known as confectioners' sugar or powdered sugar. We used

icing sugar mixture, not pure icing sugar.

Sultanas seedless white raisins.

Treacle thick, dark syrup not unlike molasses; a by-product of sugar refining. Golden syrup or honey can be substituted.

Vanilla bean dried long thin pod of vanilla orchid. The minuscule black seeds inside the bean are used to impart a vanilla flavour in baking and desserts. One bean can be used repeatedly; simply wash in warm water after use, dry well and store in airtight container.

Vanilla essence we used imitation vanilla extract.

Whisky we used a good-quality Scotch whisky.

Wine we used good-quality dry white and red wines.

Yeast allow 2 teaspoons (7g) dried granulated yeast to each 15g compressed yeast.

hundreds and thousands

jelly crystals

Choc Bits

conversion chart

MEASURES

One Australian metric measuring cup holds approximately 250ml; one Australian metric tablespoon holds 20ml; one Australian metric teaspoon holds 5ml.

The difference between one country's measuring cups and another's is within a two- or three-teaspoon variance, and will not affect your cooking results. North America, New Zealand and the United Kingdom use a 15ml tablespoon.

All cup and spoon measurements are level. The most accurate way of measuring dry ingredients is to weigh them. When measuring liquids, use a clear glass or plastic jug with the metric markings.

We use large eggs with an average weight of 60g.

DRY MEASURES

METRIC	IMPERIAL
15g	½oz
30g	1oz
60g	2oz
90g	3oz
125g	4oz (¼lb)
155g	5oz
185g	6oz
220g	7oz
250g	8oz (½lb)
280g	9oz
315g	10oz
345g	11oz
375g	12oz (¾lb)
410g	13oz
440g	14oz
470g	15oz
500g	16oz (1lb)
750g	24oz (1½lb)
1kg	32oz (2lb)

LIQUID MEASURES

METRIC	IMPERIAL
30ml	1 fluid oz
60ml	2 fluid oz
100ml	3 fluid oz
125ml	4 fluid oz
150ml	5 fluid oz (¼ pint/1 gill)
190ml	6 fluid oz
250ml	8 fluid oz
300ml	10 fluid oz (½ pint)
500ml	16 fluid oz
600ml	20 fluid oz (1 pint)
1000ml (1 litre)	1¾ pints

LENGTH MEASURES

METRIC	IMPERIAL
3mm	⅛in
6mm	¼in
1cm	½in
2cm	¾in
2.5cm	1in
5cm	2in
6cm	2½in
8cm	3in
10cm	4in
13cm	5in
15cm	6in
18cm	7in
20cm	8in
23cm	9in
25cm	10in
28cm	11in
30cm	12in (1ft)

OVEN TEMPERATURES

These oven temperatures are only a guide for conventional ovens. For fan-forced ovens, check the manufacturer's manual.

	°C (CELSIUS)	°F (FAHRENHEIT)	GAS MARK
Very slow	120	250	½
Slow	150	275-300	1-2
Moderately slow	160	325	3
Moderate	180	350-375	4-5
Moderately hot	200	400	6
Hot	220	425-450	7-8
Very hot	240	475	9

index

ARE YOU MISSING SOME OF THE WORLD'S FAVOURITE COOKBOOKS?

The Australian Women's Weekly Cookbooks are available from bookshops, cookshops, supermarkets and other stores all over the world. You can also buy direct from the publisher, using the order form below.

TITLE	RRP	QTY	TITLE	RRP	QTY
Asian, Meals in Minutes	£6.99		Japanese Cooking Class	£6.99	
Babies & Toddlers Good Food	£6.99		Kids' Birthday Cakes	£6.99	
Barbecue Meals In Minutes	£6.99		Kids Cooking	£6.99	
Beginners Cooking Class	£6.99		Lean Food	£6.99	
Beginners Simple Meals	£6.99		Low-carb, Low-fat	£6.99	
Beginners Thai	£6.99		Low-fat Feasts	£6.99	
Best Food	£6.99		Low-fat Food For Life	£6.99	
Best Food Desserts	£6.99		Low-fat Meals in Minutes	£6.99	
Best Food Fast	£6.99		Main Course Salads	£6.99	
Best Food Mains	£6.99		Mexican	£6.99	
Cakes Biscuits & Slices	£6.99		Middle Eastern Cooking Class	£6.99	
Cakes Cooking Class	£6.99		Midweek Meals in Minutes	£6.99	
Caribbean Cooking	£6.99		Muffins, Scones & Breads	£6.99	
Casseroles	£6.99		New Casseroles	£6.99	
Cheesecakes: baked and chilled	£6.99		New Classics	£6.99	
Chicken	£6.99		New Curries	£6.99	
Chicken Meals in Minutes	£6.99		New Finger Food	£6.99	
Chinese Cooking Class	£6.99		New Salads	£6.99	
Christmas Cooking	£6.99		Party Food and Drink	£6.99	
Chocolate	£6.99		Pasta Meals in Minutes	£6.99	
Cocktails	£6.99		Potatoes	£6.99	
Cooking for Friends	£6.99		Salads: Simple, Fast & Fresh	£6.99	
Cupcakes & Fairycakes	£6.99		Saucery	£6.99	
Detox	£6.99		Sauces Salsas & Dressings	£6.99	
Dinner Beef	£6.99		Sensational Stir-Fries	£6.99	
Dinner Lamb	£6.99		Short-order Cook	£6.99	
Dinner Seafood	£6.99		Slim	£6.99	
Easy Australian Style	£6.99		Stir-fry	£6.99	
Easy Curry	£6.99		Superfoods for Exam Success	£6.99	
Easy Spanish-Style	£6.99		Sweet Old Fashioned Favourites	£6.99	
Essential Soup	£6.99		Tapas Mezze Antipasto & other bites	£6.99	
French Food, New	£6.99		Thai Cooking Class	£6.99	
Fresh Food for Babies & Toddlers	£6.99		Traditional Italian	£6.99	
Get Real, Make a Meal	£6.99		Vegetarian Meals in Minutes	£6.99	
Good Food Fast	£6.99		Vegie Food	£6.99	
Great Lamb Cookbook	£6.99		Weekend Cook	£6.99	
Greek Cooking Class	£6.99		Wicked Sweet Indulgences	£6.99	
Grills	£6.99		Wok, Meals in Minutes	£6.99	
Healthy Heart Cookbook	£6.99				
Indian Cooking Class	£6.99		TOTAL COST:	£	

Mr/Mrs/Ms _____

Address _____

_____ Postcode _____

Day time phone _____ Email* (optional) _____

I enclose my cheque/money order for £ _____

or please charge £ _____

to my: ☐ Access   ☐ Mastercard   ☐ Visa   ☐ Diners Club

PLEASE NOTE: WE DO NOT ACCEPT SWITCH OR ELECTRON CARDS

Card number ☐☐☐☐☐☐☐☐☐☐☐☐☐☐☐☐☐☐

Expiry date _____ 3 digit security code *(found on reverse of card)* _____

Cardholder's name_____ Signature _____

* By including your email address, you consent to receipt of any email regarding this magazine, and other emails which inform you of ACP's other publications, products, services and events, and to promote third party goods and services you may be interested in.

To order: Mail or fax – photocopy or complete the order form above, and send your credit card details or cheque payable to: Australian Consolidated Press (UK), Moulton Park Business Centre, Red House Road, Moulton Park, Northampton NN3 6AQ, phone (+44) (0) 1604 497531 fax (+44) (0) 1604 497533, e-mail books@acpmedia.co.uk or order online at www.acpuk.com

Non-UK residents: We accept the credit cards listed on the coupon, or cheques, drafts or International Money Orders payable in sterling and drawn on a UK bank. Credit card charges are at the exchange rate current at the time of payment.

Postage and packing UK: Add £1.00 per order plus 50p per book.

Postage and packing overseas: Add £2.00 per order plus £1.00 per book.

All pricing current at time of going to press and subject to change/availability.

Offer ends 31.12.2007